# **5** VOICES

# 5 VOICES

How to Communicate
Effectively with Everyone
You Lead

JEREMIE KUBICEK    STEVE COCKRAM

WILEY

*Library of Congress Cataloging-in-Publication Data:*

Names: Kubicek, Jeremie, author. | Cockram, Steve.
Title: 5 voices : find your voice, build your team and change your world / JeremieKubicek, Steve Cockram.
Other titles: Five voices
Description: Hoboken : Wiley, 2016. | Includes index.
Identifiers: LCCN 2015037507 | ISBN 9781119111092 (hardback) ISBN 9781119111108 (ebk) | ISBN 978111911111-5 (ebk)
Subjects: LCSH: Leadership. | Self-actualization (Psychology) | BISAC:
   BUSINESS & ECONOMICS / Leadership. | SELF-HELP / Personal Growth / General.
Classification: LCC HD57.7 .K81543 2016 | DDC 658.4/092–dc23 LC record available at http://lccn.loc.gov/2015037507

Printed in the United States of America

10 9 8 7 6 5 4 3 2 1

*We dedicate this book to all of the GiANTs
who have sacrificed much, worked diligently and
served the many leaders from around the world.
This book is a testament to your diligence and
we couldn't be more excited to partner with
you to help people know themselves
so they can better lead themselves.
You are world changers!*

# Contents

# Introduction

Many people have run the gauntlet of personality tests and have come away feeling labeled as a color or a set of letters or some animal, without proper understanding of how personality wiring is mixed with historical experiences and personal choices. The truth is that we are amazingly complex people, much more so than a simple online test can show us.

All people should be able to contribute freely using their authentic, natural voices without being marginalized or maligned. Not the voice they feel they *ought to* or *should* use but the one that truly reflects who they really are. But this rarely happens. In this book, we attempt to help you do two distinctly powerful things: discover your voice and communicate more effectively.

*In this book, we attempt to help you do two distinctly powerful things: discover your voice and communicate more effectively.*

And so, we have simplified the complicated personality process by creating the 5 Voices—the Pioneer, Connector, Guardian, Creative, and Nurturer—to help you understand who you are and what it sounds like to be on the other side of your voice. We will help you explore your natural wiring along with your historical upbringing and how your personal choices affect the way you behave today. The 5 Voices gives you room to understand your voice order and explore how each different voice contributes to what people actually hear and experience. The intentional change that happens first in you will impact all those around you, whether you are a leader or simply a busy adult who wants to improve your influence and effectiveness.

Listen to Steve Cockram describing how he created the 5 Voices and the intent behind it:

As an immature Pioneer, I had no idea what it was like to be on the other side of me. Many years ago, friends of mine, Michael and Lily Newman, encouraged me to qualify in MBTI [Myers-Briggs] and Firo-B, and that began a journey of self-discovery and profound change in my own life. But while I found that I could help others grow as well, there was a twofold frustration.

First, what I was teaching was transformational for all those who engaged with it but they couldn't do it themselves. They always needed a "guru" like me to make sense of their reality. While there were financial and egotistical benefits to me in this, I always wondered whether it was possible to take the profound insights of 16 different personality wirings and repackage them in a way that kept their power but made them accessible to ordinary people, to make them simple enough to be scalable. 5 Voices was the outcome of that process, a desire to make the complex simple so that others could truly know themselves to lead themselves.

Second, I married my amazing wife Helen who turned out to be my complete opposite in every dimension of personality and wiring. Over the past 23 years we have learned to celebrate our diversity and differences but it hasn't always been easy. The 5 Voices has given us a vocabulary and language to truly understand and appreciate each other. My desire is to change the world by helping people understand each other and communicate more effectively. I truly believe there is huge, latent potential in every team and organization that remains untapped. Unleashing the full wisdom and power of the 5 Voices has the potential to change many people's worlds.

If you want to see what it looks like after someone has gone through the 5 Voices process, then read how Colonel Bill DiMarco, U.S. Air Force, describes it:

It's been an almost three-year journey now. As a military leader, I have always been fascinated with all leadership assessments, but the 5 Voices have clarified so much for both the teams I serve with and more importantly, for me.

As a Pioneer/Creative, I have always believed the status quo exists simply to be smashed. Permission is really not the issue. We can always ask for forgiveness. A strong vision for the future is the driving force toward success. The biggest insight for me is not everybody lives by the same mantra.

The aha moment when it comes to leadership is that it takes a team of all 5 Voices to truly enjoy success. Ponder DC Comic's Justice League—an amazing team of super heroes that can conquer any villain. The Justice League's real strength comes in the diversity of the team. Many comic book fans are drawn to Superman or Batman and might scoff at a hero like Aquaman, but without Aquaman the team won't get much done underwater. Consider the 5 Voices. As a Pioneer, I can establish a profound vision for the future, but without the Guardian or Nurturer, our team will quickly fall apart as we forget the needs of our people or the history, rules, and governing bodies of our organization.

Simply put, the biggest lesson as a Pioneer is to hire my weaknesses. Recently we put together a team of young leaders for mentoring purposes. I reached out to a few fellow officers to see who was interested. When we went through the 5 Voices, I was shocked to find all six had serious Pioneer, Creative, or Connector tendencies. We were missing our Guardians and Nurturers. Why? I unconsciously sought out leaders who thought like me—a huge mistake. Our conversations are a bit flat, we find we agree more than we disagree, and we see most every problem from the same vantage point.

It seems I am drawn toward those who share a strong vision for the future, but without our weaknesses represented on the team, we face certain failure. I now understand that all 5 Voices are inside of me, and I have spent a good deal of time working on my Nurturer voice—even when it feels awkward. I honestly care greatly for the people I work with, and that voice feels so hard to access at times, but practice is paramount. I have found those who are closest to me and know me best are kind, patient, and understanding when I work on my secondary voices. That is the strength of the 5 Voices and why everyone needs to understand them.

Batman needs Aquaman on the team!

## Why We Need the 5 Voices Vocabulary

For the past few years we have been teaching the 5 Voices, we have had the privilege to work with leaders in many sectors and contexts. Almost all had taken multiple personality tests before, but few could remember their results, so their "personalities" were even more confused than before because they didn't know what to do with the information they received in a one-time event. The 5 Voices have proved simple enough that everyone remembers them and can actually begin to use them from the moment they first hear about them.

And not only is this simple language of 5 Voices memorable and easy to share, it also makes transformation possible. Here is how one leader has implemented all of the 5 Voices into his organization, as an example. You'll read about many more throughout this book as well:

> I have seen major impact in my life, my family, and also at work. After learning about the foundational voices and how to access nonnatural voices, I understand more about how it feels to be on the other side of me (a Pioneer).
>
> Our whole company now speaks the 5 Voices language. This is really amazing, and I see a big transformation in our teams by using a new language and mind-set for promoting innovative leadership tools. The main change I saw in all the teams in our organization is how long-term relationships evolved in such a positive direction.

Finally, we will introduce you to a concept called the 100X Teams. This is for those serious about getting teams on the right page, becoming healthy, and then learning how to multiply that health throughout the organization or family.

Our goal here is clear. We want to help you:

1. Discover your foundational voice and learn how to master it.
2. Understand why certain voices speak and act in a certain way and give you tools to not only handle them, but help them thrive.
3. Shape your culture, communicate with clarity, and build a team that is aligned, healthy, and excels.

4. Change your personal world, from the way you communicate with your family to the way you relate to those you
   spend most of the day with.

The 5 Voices as a concept is simple yet profound. It is
designed to help you multiply healthy leadership practices and
principles throughout the whole team or organization. If you
practice it, your communication will go to another level with
everyone you lead, both at work and at home.

We hope you enjoy unpacking the truths and insights
contained within this book. It has changed our lives, it has
affected the lives of all those we have worked with around the
globe, and we believe it can impact yours, too. Let's get
started.

# SECTION 1

# The Voices of a Team

# 1

## The Voice Called Yours

For 29 years Sarah Churman could not hear. She is a wife and a mother, a friend and a daughter, and she was deaf. With an 85 bilateral decibel loss, she couldn't hear her daughter laugh or cry, the birds chirp, the door open, or her husband speak. Even more, she had never known what her own voice sounded like. Can you imagine what that must be like?

Some of our readers know this reality firsthand. According to the Hough Ear Institute, there are approximately 300 million people who suffer from a range of hearing impairment, from severe hearing loss to complete deafness. Millions of people like Sarah are not able to hear their own voice without the help of hearing aids or medicine.

Fortunately, Sarah Churman eventually received help, and with the benefit of technology, was able to experience the miracle of hearing her voice for the very first time in 2011. It is amazing to see her reaction. (Watch for yourself on You-Tube/Sarah Churman and experience the emotions of hearing your voice after 29 years of silence.)

What we are attempting to help you do in this book is, in some ways, similar to what the professionals who helped Sarah did: We want to help you hear and understand your leadership voice, maybe for the first time. We want to help you discover the power of your voice, understand what it brings at its best, and what others really hear when you speak.

Your voice is a personal trademark. It is unique because no one has experienced life the way you have. We want to help you own your voice and communicate it with a renewed sense of confidence and self-awareness.

## Hearing Your Voice for the First Time

For almost 20 years, Scott from Minnesota struggled with the gnawing feeling inside that he had nothing significant to contribute. To know Scott is to know that he is always full of ideas—ideas that could make everyone better. And yet, no one seemed to hear him or understand how his ideas could make work better for the people on his team.

Evening conversations with his wife Michelle consisted of replaying the day and hashing out the challenges he was facing, hoping to find a solution to one of his biggest questions: "How do I always find myself in the middle of two opposing opinions?" Scott was known as a kind and caring leader who could relate to others. He would share ideas with some of the leadership about how to make his teams work better, but most of the time no one would implement what seemed to him an obvious solution. He was talking, but his opinions and ideas were not being heard.

To anyone looking at Scott's life from the outside, he was the picture of a very successful salesman, rising to the top of each organization he worked for. But on the inside, something was missing. It never occurred to Scott that he had not trained his voice to be heard, and, on a deeper level, he didn't fully understand his own voice. Even more, Scott didn't understand the other voices on his team and was frustrated with his inability to bridge the gap in communication. This frustration would eventually turn to cynicism and then despair, as he began to question his own value to the team. Ultimately, the stress began to physically impact his health.

Does that sound like any of you? Anyone else feel like they are:

- Never having their ideas understood?
- Always fighting for or with people who are against the system?
- Looking at the future, while everyone else is stuck in the past?

Scott did not understand the type of leadership voice he had and what he, as a foundational voice Nurturer, could do to truly bring value to his team and family. (Note: as you will discover as you read further, we all have a foundational leadership voice that drives our actions and interactions with others. Nurturer is one of the 5 Voices.) Listen to how Scott describes finding his voice:

> After hearing the 5 Voices for the first time, I realized that I had a [leadership] voice. For many years my voice had been silent. This affected my purpose, my marriage, my team, and my organization. As I became more self-aware, I began to find my voice again. It was a hard process of going through many walls of self-preservation. I had to revive it so

it could be heard again. It has been a refining process for me. Little by little, I am becoming more and more alive to not only my voice, but also to truly understanding each of the leadership voices of those around me. Each voice needs to be heard. Part of my purpose now is helping others find their voice so they can be heard again.

Scott truly heard his voice for the first time. And our commitment to you is to help you hear yours, as well. Through the 5 Voices process you will gain an understanding of your voice, your role, and your influence in a completely new manner. We hope that reading this book will give you the opportunity to understand the way you were wired from the very beginning and that you will find this incredibly helpful in every aspect of your life.

## The Other Side of Your Voice

Do you know what it is like to be on the other side of you in a group setting? Are you aware of your tendencies and how you process information and share it? How do others tend to hear you or respond to you?

Some of us have a low speaking voice, while others have a higher pitched voice. Some of us are loud, and others are naturally quieter. It is just the way we were born. The question is, what does it feel like to be on the other side of your voice? And do you understand the power of your voice for good or ill?

The way your actual voice works is amazing. Think about this for a moment: Your vocal chords, similar to a flute, shape the air that passes through them to become an understandable sound. Your brain connects to that sound to produce words that we all understand. Amazing. In the same way that we have a physical voice, we also have a personality or leadership voice that becomes our trademark role inside organizations, families, and friendships. Through years of research and testing, we have found that there are five foundational voices that shape the daily interactions of our lives. When each individual understands what his or her voice sounds like, then they have the chance to communicate more effectively and create environments where voices that are different from their own can be truly valued and heard.

The 5 Voices are the Pioneer, the Connector, the Guardian, the Creative, and the Nurturer. By the time you have finished this book you will know which is your foundational voice and have learned to truly appreciate the contribution each of the other voices brings. You will also understand how your history and life experiences (your "nurture"), as well as your life choices, have shaped the way your voice is heard by others.

## Understanding the Code

Each of us has the ability to speak and understand all of the voices and yet, in our nature, there is always one preferred voice that is easiest for us to speak and understand. We call this our foundational voice. Some of the other voices come easily to us and are readily recognizable in the way we communicate. However, there are always one or two voices that are far harder for us to value and access. Knowing your voice order is crucial, and we will spend time later in this book assessing and understanding how to leverage and manage our voice and the voices of others.

The 5 Voices are a codebook that deciphers messages from others. Without the right cypher you will never be able to understand the intent of the original message. Our default is to interpret all communication through our own cypher (or foundational voice), which tends to be wrong a considerable amount of the time. Similarly, when we speak, we assume everyone has our codebook to interpret what we are trying to communicate. The 5 Voices, then, becomes the shared codebook that allows us to truly interpret and understand what others are trying to share, as well as to be understood ourselves.

Most relational drama and conflict comes from misunderstandings or miscommunication. When a group of people, be that in a home or workplace, is able to harness the power of the 5 Voices, tension, drama, and frustration will decrease. The 5 Voices are a common leadership language that will increase team alignment and synergy, meaning that everyone is able to relax and bring their best. You can observe how the process works in this story from Mani Joseph, a health care executive in Scotland:

> The revelatory experience for me came in accepting who I was and how I had been wired—in many ways taking the time to really get to know myself so I could begin to lead myself, to lead others, and to lead my organization. The 5 Voices showed me the patterns and trends in my past behavior, which has made it easier to take time to plan future decisions, to understand what makes me tick, and to identify those voices I respond to best as well as those that I find challenging. Identifying as a foundational voice Connector with strong Pioneer/Creative gave me legitimacy and confidence to be myself and to work on more fully understanding the contributions of Nurturers and Guardians. I am leading with renewed confidence and the team is far better placed to tackle the challenges that lie ahead.

This is what we believe will take place with you, as we first focus on you and your personal leadership journey and then the others in your life. It is vital for you to first know and understand your own voice before you begin to speculate on what others' voices might be. We cannot give what we do not possess, so together let's commit to knowing our own voice and ourselves first. Once we have done that, we can confidently and competently help others discover their own voices, and then a world of opportunity is created.

Here's one more example of the transformational experience that is possible for you. It's a story from a leader in Romania who has been implementing the 5 Voices into the IT company where she works. Marina Uliniuc shares this:

> I have to admit that the first time I interacted with the 5 Voices I was a bit suspicious; was this another box I was about to be put into? However, while some of the learning has been painful, I have learned to value those around me in a completely new way. My biggest aha was when I discovered that my tendency to ask critical questions was not always appreciated! I have started to work on my active listening, learning to draw out people's true feelings. The relational dynamics of our team have been hugely impacted by the 5 Voices; I now try to communicate enthusiasm and empathy, which I discovered they all love! This might seem common sense for a foundational voice Connector, but for the way I'm wired, as a Guardian, this was pure gold.
>
> The 5 Voices is the code that unlocks the capacity to have honest conversations and build deeper and more authentic relationships by first understanding your own voice. It will impact your teams and your families and friends only as it first impacts you.

The 5 Voices offers a competitive advantage for leaders who are able to harness its power. It doesn't matter how good your strategy is or how amazing the credentials of the people on your team. If they don't understand each other's voice and what they bring at their best, then there will always be misunderstanding, competition, and passive aggression. The 5 Voices is the code that will unlock the full capacity of your family and team. You will be able to have the honest conversations and thereby build deeper and more authentic relationships.

Whatever the reality of your current team, the 5 Voices will make you better. Knowing your own voice and how to communicate and connect with all of the other voices will take your capacity for influence and impact to the next level.

Let's now begin to understand how the 5 Voices work.

# 2

■

# How the 5
# Voices Work

There is a better way to live and to lead and to communicate. Millions of people go to their jobs with dread every day, frustrated by the other voices around them, whether it's their bosses' or their coworkers' or their clients'. Drama is mixed with inconsistent leadership and lethargy to produce a toxic work environment within the masses of teams across the world. This is what most of the world experiences.

Wouldn't it be helpful if people could begin to understand themselves and direct themselves to a more productive way of leading and living? I can hear you exclaiming now, "Absolutely, if only my boss would . . ." Let me stop you for a second and just say that it starts with you. Self-awareness creates a ripple effect as one person's positive change affects another and that person's change impacts another and so on.

Just imagine if each one of us became a master of our own voice and role and began to speak with secure, confident humility. We would have people lining up to follow us—even our kids!

The truth is that we each have a voice, and our voice can be loud and troublesome or it can be bold and helpful. We all appreciate the latter. Others of us have quiet and insecure voices, while still others have quiet and secure voices. Again, most of us would probably prefer the latter.

This process of improved self-awareness starts with each of us knowing our own voice and our tendencies and patterns as we begin to act out what is in our minds. Again, imagine if others understood what you were really trying to say most of the time. Wouldn't that be nice?

*The truth is that we each have a voice and our voice can be loud and troublesome or it can be bold and helpful.*

Listen to how this dad talks about his son:

"It makes sense now," a seasoned leader said with relief. "Now I know why I have such a hard time hearing my son. I am a Pioneer and he is a Nurturer. We speak a different language and are not hearing each other. I get it now, I am always thinking about the future, and he is always thinking about people. We have been at such odds, and now I realize that it is simply our wiring and the patterns of our voice that has brought the most consternation."

Voilà! This is what it sounds like when a humble father starts valuing the voice of his son. This is what maturity sounds like. The 5 Voices has led them to an appreciation of each other as well as given them a common language to understand one another where previously there had been nothing but frustration.

## Understanding the 5 Voices

The 5 Voices is a lens to help you see others while speaking your native tongue. It gives each of us a way to understand how we sound to others and how we interact with the world. Each voice has particular attributes that make it recognizable, as well as typical behavior tendencies, both positive and negative. All five voices are needed in organizations and groups, and one is not more important than the other. In the chapters ahead, we will describe in depth the distinguishing characteristics of each voice, but the first thing we want you to learn about the voices is that some, as you can see illustrated in Figure 2.1, are louder than others. The Pioneer is the loudest voice and the voice that can get into the red zone where volume and force of opinion are concerned. Connectors are the second loudest, followed by Guardians. Creatives and Nurturers are the quieter voices and, as you'll see, can be easily overpowered by Pioneers and Connectors.

Everyone has the capacity to use all five voices, but some of them are more natural to us than others. The voice that feels most natural is what we call our foundational voice. The other voices, which play a supporting role in the way we are heard and behave, are filtered through that primary, foundational voice, and depending on our circumstances and external influences, the predominance of those other voices can shift and become more visible at different points in our lives.

Both of us, Jeremie and Steve, have different foundational voices. Jeremie's foundational voice is Connector, while Steve's foundational voice is Pioneer. We are both quite loud, as our wives and friends can attest. Loudness is not the only distinguishing feature, but a simple reality as you begin to understand the voices, and an important one, as

5 VOICES

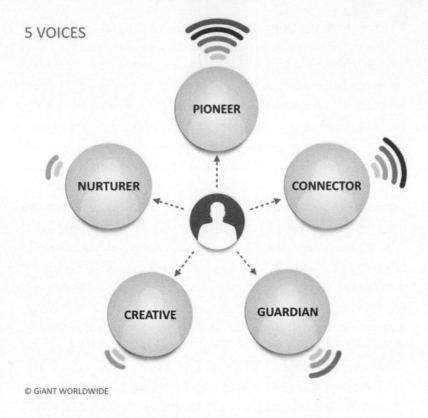

© GiANT WORLDWIDE

**Figure 2.1   5 Voices Tool**

louder voices can dominate softer ones. Remember, our goal
in sharing the 5 Voices tool is to help you know what your
voice sounds like and to help you learn to value and truly hear
the others.

As a way for you to see how the voices work, here's a short
experiment: Get a piece of paper and grab a pen. Write your
signature somewhere on your piece of paper. You probably
didn't have to think about what you were doing at all, right?
You just did it reflexively. Now, write your signature again,
but this time with the other hand. Wow, that wasn't easy, was
it? You likely had to concentrate on each letter as you wrote it

and some of your perfectionist tendencies surfaced as you tried your hardest to make the signature flow as smoothly as it does with your natural hand.

That's the best analogy to describe the voices. The first signature came from your dominant hand as you automatically picked up the pen and started writing your name. It's natural; it flows and you don't have to think about it. Of the 5 Voices, you will find there are at least two that are like your dominant hand. They're easy to access and people hear them clearly whenever you communicate. Similarly, for most of us, there are usually a couple of voices that are like our secondary hand. These voices are much more mechanical, clunky-feeling, even, and they are far harder to access because they are not natural for us. We not only find the two hard to speak ourselves, we also find them more difficult to value and engage with when we hear them. Maturity is learning to value the contribution each voice brings to the table and creating environments where each voice can be truly heard. Listen to how Diana Bocaneala, head of talent management for Endava in Cluj, Romania, describes this maturing process:

> Before understanding the 5 Voices concept, I was asking myself what was wrong with me? Why was I getting bored in discussions about feelings, or even worse, why were people telling me that I didn't understand them when I worked to solve their issues with them? After learning that my foundational voice is Pioneer, I now understand more clearly what it's like to be on the other side of my leadership. It was liberating to realize there was nothing wrong with me! I'm just different. And people around me are different as well. All the voices bring something unique and different and I'm working hard to make sure my strategic, challenging Pioneer voice doesn't dominate and overpower the other voices on my team.

This may sound easy but becoming aware of my unconscious incompetence has been painful, and I have had to apologize to a lot of people! I still don't get it right every time but I'm making progress and people are noticing it.

Your voice is vital! Whether you are in an organization or in a family, your voice represents your role, your perspective, and your contribution. Your voice is valuable when it is used for the greater good. We are going to help you discover your voice and hone it until it becomes healthy and productive for everyone around you.

## Personality Quotient

When it comes to leading or influencing, IQ is important. The unique knowledge and expertise we each possess gives us credibility with others. People like having letters after their name or plaques highlighting their credentials, identifying their skills or qualifications. These hard skills are essential to life, but in the new world you can't get away anymore with just being incredibly good at what you do.

In the new world, information is largely free. Collaboration and collective problem solving skills are increasingly more important for the success of companies than simply having high IQ employees. The new world has caused teams to need to become very dynamic, more so than at anytime in our history. Therefore, it is crucial that you relate to the people around you and leverage their skills, expertise, and knowledge for the good of the team.

Relationship management, both inside and outside organizations, is becoming more important than ever. This is one of the primary reasons we wrote *5 Gears: How to Be Present and Productive When There Is Never Enough Time*, so that we could help people learn how to connect more appropriately by being in the right gear at the right time.

However, there is one other key component to becoming a liberating leader others want to follow—the ability to know and lead yourself. We call this area PQ for personality quotient. It is your ability to become self-aware. A strong PQ allows people to ask others what it is like to be on the other side of them. PQ is actually a mirror. When you really look at yourself in a mirror you may find that you have broccoli in your teeth that no one has told you about. And we all have broccoli in our teeth. The bits of broccoli are the things about us that annoy other people the most. The 5 Voices, then, is actually a mirror to help you improve your PQ to become more self-aware than you ever have been before.

## Nature, Nurture, Choice

Most of you reading this will have gone through a personality inventory at some point in your life and come away labeled in some fashion—a badger, a white with a blue spot, a D, an INFP, an ESTJ, and so on. There are so many personality tests out there, and in our opinion they claim far more than they are really able to deliver. It's important to remember that, at their best, they give you a snapshot of your current leadership behaviors. However, any attempt to extrapolate definitive truths from an online assessment and tell people who they are, massively underestimates the complexity of human behavior. There is more to our behavior than just our personality tendencies.

Our leadership behaviors, which is what people actually experience being on the other side of us, are shaped by three equal components: nature, nurture, and choice.

Nature is the first part. Some of us were born with blue eyes and some with brown. We are short or tall, right handed or left handed, and so on. Your genes are what they are. You can't alter the eye color you were born with any more than you can change your personality wiring. Whether we come into the world as introverts or extroverts, thinkers or feelers, we are who we are. Understanding your nature, and how those built-in strengths and weaknesses impact your leadership behaviors is hugely important, but it's only one-third of the equation.

Nurture is the second part and it's tricky, because looking at it requires us to review the key life events, authority figures, and experiences that have shaped us.

Whether we realize it or not, we have been shaped by a wide variety of external influences, ranging from our parents and teachers, to our successes and failures, to the culture of the communities where we live. Perhaps you can recall a teacher from high school who raised the bar and empowered you to reach beyond yourself or a manipulative boss who left you feeling marginalized and undervalued. All of our experiences, for better or worse, the expectations of others and the social norms where we live often create a sense within us that we "ought" to do this or "should" do that (see Figure 2.2). And those presumptions affect our behavior and alter the way we lead.

The choices we make are the last component that shapes our behavior. We spend our lives making choices, and by the time we are well into adulthood, we all can point to the choices we've made that have been life-giving, good decisions, as well as the fair share of choices that, given the chance, we might not make a second time. Like Pavlov's learned response, whether good or bad, our choices impact our behavior.

OUGHTS AND SHOULDS OF NURTURE

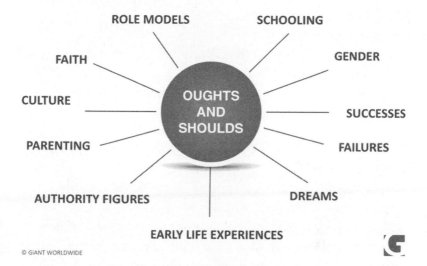

© GiANT WORLDWIDE

**Figure 2.2   Oughts and Shoulds of Nurture**

You can picture the man deciding whether to venture out on his own or stay with the company he has worked at for over 18 years. His choice has ramifications, as in the famed Clash song, "Should I stay or should I go? If I stay there will be trouble; if I go it will be double." When a person chooses to stay put because of the responsibilities that he has to his wife and kids, a part of his soul dies, and yet venturing out to follow some dream can be dangerous. The choices we make affect dozens, maybe hundreds of people in our lives.

In the end, what people see and experience on the other side of our leadership behaviors is a complex mix of nature, nurture, and choice. Each of us truly is unique; personality assessments are two-dimensional and don't have the capacity to separate out how the individual components of nature, nurture, and choice are truly shaping your leadership behaviors. However, it is possible to understand our essential nature, to see how nurture has played its role in shaping us, and review the choices we have made along the way. Such insights allow us

> *Our leadership behavior is a complex mix of nature, nurture, and choice. Each of us truly is unique.*

to more fully comprehend our voice, which is precisely what we plan to do in the coming chapters.

## Know Yourself, Lead Yourself

In light of that, we share a health warning before we proceed: 5 Voices is not trying to label you or tell you definitively who you are (your nature). We are offering a simple yet profound lens that will allow you to observe your leadership behaviors and the behaviors of those around you in a new light. Our experience has been that the more we know ourselves, the greater our capacity to truly lead ourselves and others well.

We all have tendencies, whether we're aware of them or not. Those tendencies create patterns of behavior that shape our actions. Actions always have consequences in every reality of our lives—self, family, team, organization, and community. Here's a great example of this from Steve.

Once my wife said to me, 'Stephen, you have a tendency to go into social events and look for the most interesting, attractive, exciting people, anyone who can add to the sum of your knowledge and expertise and desire to master the world, and you spend all your time with them. If there's nobody like that in the room, you look around to see if you can provoke an argument, just for the sheer joy of intellectual sparring, and if you can't find anyone to debate with, you either leave, fall asleep in the corner, or get your phone out.' Ouch. That hurts, but it was true of me then. Some of you may have similar tendencies. That was the 'broccoli in my teeth'; I didn't realize I was doing it and therefore couldn't lead myself because of my lack of self-awareness. That tendency created an ingrained pattern of behavior that shaped my actions, but I didn't know it. And it had consequences that shaped my reality and reduced my influence. So here's the little nugget of truth: Your tendencies don't go away. (It's really annoying to hear that, I know.) I still have that tendency, but I know myself well enough to know I don't want to be defined by that pattern of behavior. So now I watch myself and I hear myself. The trigger for me is when I'm starting to create an argument. And then I decide that I don't want to be defined by that tendency. I look around the room to find the person who probably feels most insecure about being in that room, and I use all of my skills, knowledge, and expertise to help make this the best evening that he's ever had. I'm going to find out everything I can about that person and I'm going to serve him to the very best of my abilities. (So if I ever meet you at a party and come up to you to talk, you'll always wonder which camp you fit into!) This is an example of how to become self-aware and to know how your behaviors affect those around you. It turns out that the behaviors I described were being driven primarily by my pioneering nature. My parents had always modeled sacrificial love and service for those on the margins so I couldn't blame my nurture! Once I became aware of these negative tendencies I made a conscious choice to change them. We all have idiosyncrasies and tendencies that undermine our influence without us knowing. We simply want to help you deal with those issues through the 5 Voices so that you can learn to change your patterns and benefit from productive actions that lead to positive outcomes.

The 5 Voices, then, is a very simple tool to understand, but it is challenging to implement because of our own tendencies.

Audrey Frey from Atlanta, Georgia, shares this insight on using the 5 Voices in her new management role:

> I think the greatest area of growth as it relates to the 5 Voices is realizing that they even exist. Prior to learning this tool, while I wasn't aware of it, I think I believed that everyone thought and communicated just as I did. Learning the 5 Voices has shown me that we all communicate differently, and it is important to evaluate a variety of different cues to really hear and understand the message being communicated. One of my biggest ahas is that most people are unaware of the unspoken messages they are relaying to people who may speak in a different voice. I've learned not to take things so personally and am much more patient and less judgmental of others who communicate in a different foundational voice than my own.

## How the 5 Voices Were Created

The research of Carl Jung has had significant ripple effects in the areas of psychology and human development. Isabel Myers and Katherine Briggs found Jung's work and built the most widely used instrument (the Myers–Briggs Type Indicator) to understand personality type with a focus on the nature of a person, their personality and wiring, their nurture, their experiences, and the inputs from their life that affect their behaviors.

Others have been building or innovating on their work. For example, take the recent emergence of Socionics, the integration of Carl Jung's type theory with what is called information metabolism (i.e. how people select and process information) to provide some fresh insight and application across a number of disciplines. Some significantly smart and talented guys have created something very fascinating, but not very scalable.

At GiANT, we have been working with leaders, teams, and organizations of all stripes for over a decade and have a passion (bordering on obsession) for helping people in ways that are simple, scalable, and sustainable. As a result, we have taken Jungian typology and looked at how we could make this valuable, transformative information even more accessible and helpful for those we are serving. We utilized the insights from basic personality typings as well as what is known as type dynamics to distill the roles within a team down to five distinct voices: the Pioneer, Connector, Creative, Guardian, and Nurturer.

We have taken thousands of leaders from all over the world through the 5 Voices to provide something that actually works over the long term, as it is easily understood and owned by individuals at all levels. It works. It is clear, concise, and highly practical as these leaders can attest. Hear how Ryan Underwood, a CEO in Tulsa, Oklahoma, describes connecting with a Guardian:

> Personally, 5 Voices has helped me understand relationships with two of my Guardians. I'm a Creative and over the years we've had this odd on and off working relationship. When we are on, there is no place I'd rather be when it comes to leading our company. When we are off, I can't get far enough away from them. But, now I know why this happens. What I do after building something really important is to call in my Guardians to literally protect the work, the innovation, the client relationship. And they are masterful at this! I could walk away for months or even years and come back and see a beautiful process in place just as we had left off.

However, our relationship would get off track when I would come back in to help (as I saw it then!), innovate, or change something in their world. And, often I would do so without recognizing or acknowledging the tremendous work they had already done. I did not realize how disruptive and frustrating my behavior was to them; in my mind, I was only trying to help and expected them to be grateful. Their critical questions, desire for a detailed Gantt chart, and apparent risk aversion used to feel so negative. Now I know it was their way of making sure they could effectively deliver the change.

When people begin to understand their foundational voice, and the voices that they are resistant to, they begin to become more effective in their communication and in their patience and connectivity.

In the next chapter, you will have the chance to take the 5 Voices assessment and begin to more fully understand the power of your voice. You will also begin to understand and engage with the other voices among which you live and work each day. Ultimately, our hope is that this tool will allow you to know yourself, lead yourself, and become the leader that you have always wanted to be.

Are you ready to discover your voice and all the benefits that come with it?

# 3

■

# Discovering
# Your Voice

The 5 Voices self-assessment is simple. Taking it won't make you break into a cold sweat the way we did when we were taking placement tests for university. No calculators or extra pencils needed. We just ask for you to open your mind and be in responsive mode to the information that follows so you can determine which voice is foundational for you and embrace it confidently.

We are going to help you to order your voices from your foundational voice (first voice) to your nemesis voice (last voice). In the end you will learn how this voice order affects your behavior and will help you understand yourself and then other people. So, whether you are a Pioneer, Connector, Guardian, Creative, or Nurturer, we want to help you know yourself so that you can lead yourself.

Knowing your voice implies that you understand who you are and how you contribute in life in the best possible way. Knowing your voice means identifying your natural gifts and abilities. Appreciating your voice gives you the freedom to be who you are, which, in turn, enables you to respect others in your life and extend the same freedom to them.

## Assumptions

Before you begin your assessment to determine your foundational voice and voice order, it is important to understand these six realities:

1. We all have a leadership voice, which is what others experience on the other side of us. It's made up of a complex mix of the five separate voices.
2. We each have the capacity to use all five of the voices. You are not limited to one. We need them all and have the capacity to speak them all, and we already do to a varying degree, but some of them are more natural to us than others.
3. You have a foundational voice that is your nature. What others experience being on the other side of you may change over the years because of your nurture and choices, but you have a natural voice order with a foundational voice through which every other voice is heard. Remember the analogy about your right and left hands? We use both hands but one of them comes more naturally to us. It's the same with the voices. There is an order in which you are comfortable using them, and they shape what it is that people hear.
4. Maturity allows us to value the contribution each voice brings. Nature, nurture, and choice have all played a part in shaping your voice. The immature leader or person will

only value the voices he finds most natural and discount the voices of others. We are seeking to help you evolve in the way you live and lead, so your maturity is a goal here.

5. Don't assume you know what someone else's foundational voice is. Remember, we are complex people covered up by our experiences and choices whether as mature or immature people. Thus, it is difficult to definitively predict a person's foundational voice. Remember, also, that we all suffer those oughts and shoulds, and it is very easy to put people in a box, or assign a particular identity, that is not, in fact, accurate. If they've assumed a particular role early in life, and then continued in that way, what you see in their leadership behavior may simply be the result of nurture and choice rather than their nature.

6. Don't assume you know what each word means. The definitions of each voice are important and specific. When we say Creative, we do not mean graphic designer or artist alone; it is much more profound than this. The same is true for Guardian and Pioneer and the other voices. You will associate certain definitions with these voices, but we are asking you to be careful to use the definitions and common language we have refined over the years for the 5 Voices, rather than your original preconceptions, which might be misleading.

Lastly, some encouragement to be open minded as you dig in: When teaching about the 5 Voices we have found that some people can be critical of what they see in the mirror. Some of you will see yourself or hear your voice for the first time and you may not like it. "Do I really sound like that?" may be a common question of yours for a while. And that's okay. We want to assure you that while we are helping you to identify your foundational voice and associated tendencies, we are not trying to make you feel boxed in or that you are a negative person. It's actually the opposite: We are trying to help you to discover your voice so that you can be the best version of you.

We all have tendencies and those tendencies, based on our wiring, create patterns of behavior that over time can stick and start to define our actions. The more we understand and know ourselves, the greater our capacity to choose our actions in order to define our reality. Rather than just being defined by our tendencies, "Oh, that's Steve. He's just like that," which sounds like an excuse, we want you to know what your tendencies are so you can leverage the ones that are helpful and lessen the ones that create pain points in your relationships. We want you to be self-aware so your reality is the one you actually choose.

## 5 Voices Assessment

Now, with these realities in hand, you're ready for your 5 Voices self-assessment. The process and instructions are simple and follow a color-coded system to rank each voice. The goal is for you to list your voice order from your foundational voice to your nemesis voice (the one hardest for you to speak or relate to). The color-coding is relatively simple. Think about the definition for each voice and consider if it's an easy voice or difficult voice for you to hear and value in others. You'll be assigning each voice a color based on how you rank it (see Figure 3.1).

Green means, "Wow, I totally connect with this voice. I hear and speak it easily. This is really my foundational voice." And, it's your default pattern of communicating and thinking.

Yellow means, "I get it, but I have to think about how to speak and hear it. It's not an automatic connection for me." This is not your foundational voice, but you've learned how to value it and access it, so you can use it when needed and

HOW TO RATE YOUR VOICE

**GREEN**
▸ My Foundational Voice, my default pattern
  of communication & thinking

**YELLOW**
▸ Not my Foundational Voice but I value it
  and it's easily accessible

**RED**
▸ Not my Foundational Voice, I find it hard to
  value and hard to access

© GIANT WORLDWIDE

**Figure 3.1    Rate Your Voice**

know how to draw it out from other people in a group or team environment.

Red means, "Nope. Sounds like a foreign language to me. I don't hear it at all." Not only is a red voice not your foundational voice, you will struggle sometimes to access it, and you may find it hard to value it in others. We call that the nemesis voice.

Now, for those readers already panicked about being labeled, we are giving you the option to add shading to your primary colors. For instance, you might have a voice that seems to you to be more like green with a hint of yellow, or a voice that is yellow with a tinge of red, and so forth. If you need a range of colors to get a more accurate picture of your voice order, no problem; we're giving you seven choices. Just remember the assessment is about giving you an idea of how familiar and comfortable that voice is for you and, by extension, what your leadership tendencies might be. In the end, we simply want you to be able to rank the voices from 1-5.

Beginning with the Nurturer, we'll give you a definition for each voice. The self-assessment, which we've broken into four specific areas, will follow each definition and will help you understand:

1. What the voice sounds like.
2. What they bring at their best.
3. What questions they are really asking.
4. What the potential negative impact could be.

You will have an opportunity at the end of each section to determine if the voice is a foundational or nemesis voice for you, using our color-coding system, as well as rank your voices. In the chapters that follow the self-assessment, we'll examine each of the 5 Voices in greater depth.

Let's get started! We'll begin with the Nurturer.

## Nurturer

All of the voices are naturally hardwired to do certain things well. For Nurturers, that thing is caring for others and helping to develop the people around them. Whatever the context of the relationship, be it family, work, or the larger community, Nurturers are amazing keepers of relationships and defenders of values. In the same way engine oil is essential for a car to run well, so too is the Nurturer voice necessary in building and maintaining relationships. Focused on the here and now, Nurturers make it a priority to know what the people in their circle of care need and value, and their innate desire for relational harmony gives them an intuitive ability to understand what to do to meet those needs, both spoken and unspoken. Nurturers tend to have quieter voices and can be drowned out and bullied by other louder voices. As such, Nurturers can begin to question their value when they don't feel heard. Groups and teams suffer without the contribution of secure, confident Nurturers, and those who lead Nurturers must provide an environment where they feel safe to contribute their best.

### *Are You a Nurturer?*

- Nurturers are champions of people and work to take care of everyone around them.
- They are always concerned about the relational health and harmony of the group.
- They are completely committed to protecting values and principles.
- Nurturers have a hard time separating their work from who they are.
- They innately understand how certain actions, behaviors, or initiatives will affect people.

#### *What Do They Bring At Their Best?*

- Nurturers appreciate each person's contribution and voice.
- They intuitively feel how an organization will react to a new idea.
- Nurturers are pragmatic realists—they want to make sure that decision makers have really thought things through.
- They defend values—people come before profit.
- Nurturers function as the relational oil inside the organization.
- They have a commitment to relational harmony before/ during/after meetings.

#### *What Questions Are They Really Asking Inside?*

- "What are people around me going to be most upset about?" This occurs because the Nurturer looks out for others and cares for them as family.
- "Are the leaders really thinking about the people's best interests?"

- "Don't others see how people are upset by this decision?" Because Nurturers take care of others they wonder if others think like they do.
- "Do the leaders want to hear what I think?" Nurturers don't believe that what they have to say is valued as much as it actually is.

*Negative Impact*
- Nurturers can be overly resistant to change and can be passive aggressive.
- They can feel unable to challenge a proposed direction when they disagree.
- Making money is often seen as an impure motive.
- Nurturers don't usually value the contribution they make.

Considering the definition and detail of the Nurturer voice, what color is it for you right now? Note: By "right now," we mean assess your current leadership behaviors today, as a snapshot of your current reality, reflecting all your personal growth and development up until now.

Is it:

- Green?
- Green with a hint of yellow?
- Yellow with a hint of green?
- Yellow?
- Yellow with a hint of red?
- Red with a hint of yellow? Or,
- Red?

Write down what color this voice is for you.

**Creative**

The Creative voice is another quiet voice that can be hard to hear, especially when in the presence of loud, opinionated voices like the Connectors and Pioneers. The Creative genius, which possesses an extraordinary gift for visioning the future, can easily be missed. Creatives are amazing conceptual architects and love scanning the horizon; they are often drawn to new trends in ideas and technology. They come equipped with an early warning radar system that gives them the ability to sense danger where values run the risk of being compromised, and they can see opportunities, solutions, and possibilities for the future long before they become reality. The Creative voice invariably prefers to listen and process other contributions internally before responding. When asked for input, often their first thoughts come out in a way that others find confusing or even critical—they need others to invest time, asking them clarifying questions, which gives them the space to allow the right answer to surface. When other voices are patient in this process, they will be amazed at the gold a Creative is able to contribute. Creatives are invariably idealists and internal perfectionists who also have a strong social conscience. Creatives need to know it's safe to share their ideas; if they get shot down too often, or judged on their initial input, they will stop bringing their best.

### Are You a Creative?

- Creatives are champions of innovation and future ideas.
- They are conceptual architects and are able to see how all the pieces fit together.
- Creatives are never satisfied with the status quo; they always believe it can be better. The word "*can't*" is not in their vocabulary.
- Creatives long for an environment where they know their contribution is valued and appreciated.
- They are purists in their minds and want to see their ideas become reality.

*What Do They Bring At Their Best?*

- Creatives see the future first, both in terms of long-term opportunities and potential dangers.
- Because they are never satisfied with good enough, they push organizations and people to higher heights.
- They are like an "early warning radar system" and can see the opportunities and dangers of the future before everyone else.
- Creatives have the capacity to think outside the box.
- They have a strong social conscience and a desire for organizational integrity.

*What Questions Are They Really Asking Inside?*

- "So what? Does all this activity really get us closer to our vision?" Because the Creative has the master plan in their mind they want to make sure the activities lead to that plan.
- "Why do people never seem to fully understand my ideas?" They get frustrated when others say things that they believe they have already said.
- "Are we compromising our values in a way that we might regret later?"
- "Are you a safe person for me to share my ideas with?" Creatives don't like to share their ideas where they won't be valued.
- "Why are we limiting ourselves?"
- "How could we do it better?"

*Negative Impact*

- They can often fail to celebrate the 90% that has been achieved, focusing instead on the 10% that hasn't been accomplished yet.
- Idealism can often trump pragmatism, leading to a sense of paralysis until the Creative believes it can be perfect.
- Creatives have a tendency to ignore financial constraints and other practical hurdles.

For the Creative voice, ask yourself the same thing: "How familiar is this voice to me? How much does this define the way I communicate right now, the way I engage with others?"

Is it:

- Green?
- Green with a hint of yellow?
- Yellow with a hint of green?
- Yellow?
- Yellow with a hint of red?
- Red with a hint of yellow? Or,
- Red?

Write down what color this voice is for you.

## Guardian

By their very nature, Guardians are wired to preserve and protect. Their voice is louder, though not the loudest, and Guardians exist to ensure that what is already established is not going to be lost as the more future-orientated voices seek adventure on new frontiers. Like the Nurturer, Guardians are present-oriented; they like to ask detailed, analytical, and critical questions. They are not afraid to address tough or awkward issues, and, unless they are convinced, you can expect Guardians to put the brakes on when it comes to any kind of change where money, energy, or other resources could be potentially lost or wasted. Though they dislike compromise and have to beware of their tendency to interrogate, no one can deliver projects on time or on budget like a Guardian.

### *Are You a Guardian?*

- Guardians are champions of responsibility and stewardship.
- They respect and value logic, systems, order, procedure, and process.

- They seek clarity, as well as logical and proven decision-making criteria even if they have to ask the tough questions to get there.
- Guardians like to see established track records of success to justify trying something different.
- They can feel frustrated that they are sometimes seen as "raining on the parade" just because they are trying to make sure the team makes the best decision possible.

## What Do They Bring At Their Best?

- The Guardian has a relentless commitment to ask the difficult questions, especially if they feel that no one else will.
- They have a selfless capacity to deliver the vision once it has been agreed.
- Guardians have a long-term commitment to deliver on time and on budget.
- They are the custodians of resources and how money is invested/spent, acting as if it is their own money.
- They have the ability to detach decision-making from personal sentiments.
- Guardians guard what is already working.

## What Questions Are They Really Asking Inside?

- "Is this worth the risk and investment?" Guardians always remember the time where money or time was misspent on some harebrained idea and want to make sure that doesn't happen again.
- "Convince me that change is really necessary."
- "Can we test the hypothesis before we go all in?" Guardians like pilot programs so they can test the idea before fully committing.
- "Am I at risk of being taken advantage of?" Most Guardians have stories about the last time they fell for some charismatic speaker or grandiose idea and they choose to not do that again.
- "Are we honoring the past as we look towards the future?"

*Negative Impact*

- An immature Guardian is often slow to compromise when they have a strongly held opinion. They can be stubborn.
- They have a deep desire for truth and right decisions, which can often override the feelings of others.
- Guardians can appear overly critical of people and ideas.
- They can interrogate people and lose influence because of their negative response to ideas.
- Tone and tact can often be an issue for a Guardian. They often don't see what it is like to be on the other side of them.

The Guardian comes to most relational engagements with a slightly different agenda than the previous two voices we've heard about. See where you are in your assessment.

Is it:

- Green?
- Green with a hint of yellow?
- Yellow with a hint of green?
- Yellow?
- Yellow with a hint of red?
- Red with a hint of yellow? Or,
- Red?

As before, determine what color this voice is and write it down.

## Connector

The Connector voice is the next loudest voice in succession from the Guardian and best recognized as someone who is a genius at connecting people and their aspirations to ideas and resources. The quintessential people person, expect someone with a foundational Connector voice to have a large number of close friends and to always make contacts and new relationships everywhere she goes. Known for their charisma and gift for being persuasive messengers, you can be sure that Connectors will do their level best to encourage everyone to buy into whatever they are excited about. Though focused on the big picture of the future, Connectors have an intuitive ability to sense what others feel and need in the moment, which is what gives them their uncanny ability to connect people to opportunities. Connectors have to beware of their need to receive credit for their ideas and their tendency to be people pleasers, but when they are healthy, affable, and resourceful Connectors are a unifying force in a group or on a team.

### Are You a Connector?

- Connectors are champions of relationships and strategic partnerships.
- They rally people around causes and things they believe in.
- Connectors believe in a world where everyone can play and get excited about future opportunities . . . and they work to make it happen.
- Receiving appreciation and credit for making key connections is highly motivating and energizing for Connectors.
- Connectors often respond to challenges with: "Whatever we need, I can get it or I have a source."

### What Do They Bring At Their Best?
- Connectors have the capacity to maintain a large number of relationships.
- They know how to connect people to their own aspirations.

- Connectors have boundless Creativity, Energy, and Imagination.
- They create connections to new opportunities and networks.
- They are usually persuasive and inspirational communicators.

*What Questions Are They Really Asking Inside?*
- "What will make this idea really connect with people?"
- "You really can't 'see it'?" This happens when they are explaining an idea and the other person rejects it or discounts it.
- "Is everyone still with me?" Connectors want everyone to buy in.
- "Are you aware of what I've done?" Accomplishments are a big deal to Connectors and they want to make sure you are at least aware.

*Negative Impact*
- Connectors can be people pleasers and therefore not bring needed challenge.
- When they feel critiqued they sell harder rather than understand why the other person may not be interested.
- Oftentimes the Connector won't hear or engage fully with critical feedback.
- Connectors can boomerang conversations by hijacking them and making the conversations be about them instead of the other person.
- The immature Connector can oftentimes become passive aggressive with a person who seems to reject them, and becomes vindictive.

Remember, we are trying to list the 5 Voices in order of strongest to weakest as they pertain to you. How strong is your Connector voice? Ponder where this and the other voices fall in your natural voice order.

Is it:

- Green?
- Green with a hint of yellow?
- Yellow with a hint of green?
- Yellow?
- Yellow with a hint of red?
- Red with a hint of yellow? Or,
- Red?

Write down what color this voice is for you.

## Pioneer

We've saved the most dominant and loudest voice, the Pioneer, for last. If you are a Pioneer, you may not enjoy going last, as going first, being first, being out in front is a primary characteristic of the Pioneer and, indeed, where Pioneers function at their very best. With eyes and mind focused on the horizon, the Pioneer is always gunning for the next big breakthrough. With an unparalleled ability to think strategically, Pioneers are experts at aligning people, systems, and resources to deliver big-picture visions. And although hard charging and quite opinionated, they have a gift for painting a compelling vision of the future and inviting people to be at their table. Their motto is invariably, "Go big or go home," and although their big ideas are what launch new companies, great products, or the next big adventure, if they want people to be part of their experience, they have to be mindful of the strength of their voice and critique.

The vocabulary of 5 Voices is beneficial in understanding the relative strengths of people and therefore in proactively leading them, whether at home, in the community, or at work. When this language begins to take root it becomes easier to have the honest conversations as people begin to understand the context of each voice and speak to the voice with clarity.

## Are You a Pioneer?

- Pioneers are champions of aligning people with resources to win or achieve the objective.
- They approach life with an "Anything is possible!" attitude.
- Pioneers believe visioning a new future is always the highest priority.
- They are always seeking to find the quickest, fastest, and most efficient way to do things.
- Pioneers value "outside the box thinking," interesting or different ways of doing things, and tend to seek out the most interesting people to learn from and add to their body of knowledge.

### What Do They Bring At Their Best?
- Pioneers bring strategic military-like thinking to achieve the agreed objective.
- They display the courage to make difficult decisions and prioritize the vision.
- Pioneers communicate an attractive vision of the future with confidence.
- The Pioneer has the capacity to align resources and people to make things happen.
- They have the tenacity, energy, and strong desire for the team to win.

### What Questions Are They Really Asking Inside?
- "Who says we can't?" They actually want to know names so they can decide if they want them on their team or not.
- "Do you really not 'get it'?" If you don't, then you will not be in their inner circle.
- "Are you competent?" Pioneers want the best people around the table.

- "Have you got a proven track record?" Pioneers love to be around people who have already succeeded in something.

*Negative Impact*
- They can appear arrogant with a "me-focused" agenda at times.
- Immature Pioneers fail to hear or value all of the 5 Voices.
- They quickly get frustrated with those who don't "get it."
- Pioneers exude a "back me or fight me!" mentality when they present their ideas.
- They can drive too hard with an insensitivity to the needs of others.
- Because they separate business from personal they can hurt people by their tone and tact and not realize it.

Pioneers don't like being last, as we explained in the definition; however, it is our final voice to assess. Take a look at these points and decide where your Pioneer voice is.

Is it:

- Green?
- Green with a hint of yellow?
- Yellow with a hint of green?
- Yellow?
- Yellow with a hint of red?
- Red with a hint of yellow? Or
- Red?

Write down what color this voice is for you.

You are finished. Good job! Any assessment, whether it's an online questionnaire or a self-assessment, which is what you just did, tells you your current leadership behaviors. Remember, your leadership behaviors are made up of your nature, which is your wiring; and your nurture, the external environment that has shaped you; as well as the choices that you've made.

## Voice Order

Now, let's take what you just learned and create a ranked order of your voices. Rank the one or two green voices as numbers one and two, and rank the rest in order from the ones that are your strongest and easiest to access and value to the least. For example, Jeremie's voice order is:

1. Connector
2. Pioneer
3. Creative
4. Nurturer
5. Guardian

Steve is very similar to Jeremie. His voice order is:

1. Pioneer
2. Connector
3. Creative
4. Guardian
5. Nurturer

Now, list your voice order.

1.
2.
3.
4.
5.

Remember, your whole voice is not just one but a combination of all the voices filtered through the lens of your strongest, foundational voice. Steve may be a Pioneer by nature, but you'll hear Connector, you'll hear Creative, hopefully you might hear a little bit of Nurturer and a little bit of Guardian. Maturity as a leader, then, is, the ability to understand your voice and lead yourself to be a help to others rather than be a nuisance. It's working to intentionally grow in all your voices and learning to truly value the contribution each brings to the table. Here, Ryan Underwood from Tulsa, Oklahoma, shares his ahas:

> I had taken and even facilitated numerous personality and leadership assessments over my 20-plus-year career. Prior to understanding the 5 Voices, my approach was one of "awareness" of other styles, the situations when people are at their natural best, and how I interacted with them. However, the next level of leadership maturity is realizing that *you*—each of us—have within us all 5 Voices and that we are born with a foundational voice and one or two others that are relatively easy for us to access. However, the aha has been to understand that I have two voices, Nurturer and Guardian, that are much harder for me to value and access. My goal is to be a mature leader who has learned how to truly value all of the 5 Voices and create the context where each member of my team is able to bring their best to the table.

It is vital to understand your foundational voice and your voice order as we move from assessment to application. In the next chapters we are going to unpack each voice at a deeper level, so that you can fully appreciate your own voice and begin to value the voices of others in your life, whether your family, friends, or team.

# 4

# The Nurturer
# Voice

We'll begin our in-depth exploration of each of the 5 Voices with the Nurturer, the voice of the people. Nurturers are the champions of relational harmony and oil the gears of relationships in groups. Naturally wired to put others' needs ahead of their own, Nurturers thrive in environments where courtesy and respect for others are second nature.

As people who are present-oriented, Nurturers take care of things today that will affect others tomorrow. They are the voice that champions values inside organizations. The Nurturer is the manager who doesn't just quote the values but lives them, the teacher who goes the extra mile to support the student above and beyond the normal expectation, the friend who puts her own plans on hold when she senses the needs of another. In a word, Nurturers are caretakers.

Healthy Nurturers make the most amazing leaders as they have an unparalleled ability to make others feel valued and included. The Nurturer might be a CEO who has created a business that serves people or the coach who helps develop the student-athlete's character and academics along with his sport. They are men and they are women. They are the leaders who focus on creating a family atmosphere at work, or the parents who make sure that their kids have everything they need to start school, down to the sandwich sliced "just so" in the lunch box. Nurturers take delight in remembering the small details that matter to those they care for at home and at the office, and where other voices have to work hard to remember these niceties, Nurturers do this instinctively and effortlessly. Theirs is the voice that ensures people are not only taken care of but that they are thriving inside the organization.

We need the Nurturer voice in every organization, family, or group of people. Without it, the needs of people will be neglected or deferred for tasks or budgets. Nurturers themselves, however, can be overlooked or feel undervalued because they tend to be quieter voices. A large majority of people inside organizations are Nurturers. In fact, 43 percent of the population at large has Nurturer as its foundational voice, which accounts for the largest percentage of all the voices. Even more, 70 percent of all Nurturers are women. Imagine that. That means that 30 percent of the entire population are female Nurturers, or put another way, 6 out of 10 women speak Nurturer as their foundational voice.

As a quick reminder, each of us has the ability to speak all of the voices, but not all are as easy to hear and value for each of us. The voice that is most natural to us is called our foundational voice. This is important to note, as some of you scored high for Nurturer, while others scored much lower. The goal of this book is to help you not only identify your foundational voice but increase your ability to understand those voices that are different from yours and harder to hear.

Nurturers at their core are all about taking care of people. Here is a great example of what a Nurturer sounds like. Listen to Amy Norton, from Nashville, Tennessee, share what she's learned about herself:

> It's been a game changer for me to embrace what it means to be a Nurturer. The language of the 5 Voices in many ways has validated who I am and allowed me to be authentically me. I no longer feel the need to apologize for being sensitive. I recognize my ability to feel deeply, to sense the needs of others, and to see and manage all the small details that go hand-in-hand with being a present-oriented caregiver. On a team, my voice is needed to help make the future-oriented visionary's dream a reality. Nurturers are the small pebbles that fill in the empty spaces around the big rocks and help complete the mosaic, whatever that is— family, business opportunity, the wider community. We help hold everything, and everyone, together on the journey. We're necessary, not optional, and discovering this fact has been a gift. I'll paraphrase a funny quote I saw on Facebook that sums up how I see my role in the world now through the lens of the 5 Voices: "I'm not insulted if you call me sensitive. Empathy is my superpower!"

All of the voices have some attributes that make them distinct and equip them to play a unique role in a group or on a team. For a Nurturer, as we've seen, it's all about people, relational harmony, and values. To fully understand what this means, we'll dig deeper and explore what Nurturers are really thinking, what they bring at their best, questions they're really asking, and what's the negative impact of the voice to the team or family or friends when they function in an immature way.

## What They Are Thinking

What do you suppose a Nurturer is thinking most of the day? What drives them when they wake up in the morning? If we are to understand the Nurturer behavior we need to understand how they think.

For a Nurturer, there is a desire for everyone to treat each other with respect. It's always personal. Every comment or conversation or employee review is personal. That is how they are wired. Therefore, they are always asking themselves if the person in front of them values them and is for them. "Does she respect me? Does he value what I have to say?" If not, Nurturers will tend to pull back or stay silent, as they become skeptical about the other person's motives.

The Nurturer wants discussions or debates to be carried out with civility. They want teammates or family members to consider the impact decisions will have on all of those involved. They are constantly thinking, "If so-and-so goes and does this-or-that like he did last week, it's going to be really painful for so-and-so." Nurturers watch other relational interactions and they will look at some of the other voices that are much less sensitive or more harsh and wonder, "Do they have to do that? Do they not know what damage they are doing?"

Foundational voice Nurturers think about today more than tomorrow. They are focused on the here and now and think a lot about the issues of the day and the details that affect others in their lives. They can get fixated on the specifics and miss the big picture, so growth for the Nurturer is learning how to use their strength in a healthy way and always to connect back to the vision.

On a personal level, the Nurturer simply wants the opportunity to share in a safe environment. All Nurturers wonder whether they should be leaders around the table, whether there's somebody else who's better than they are, whether this is a safe and affirming environment in which they can contribute. They see the Pioneers with their strategies for global domination, the Connectors sharing about all the people they know, and the Creatives discussing their ground-breaking research. Nurturers wonder if they have what it takes to play at the same level. Their unspoken desire, then, is for relational harmony. "Is it safe to share here? Will they really listen to me?"

## What They Bring at Their Best

What Nurturers bring at their best is that they, more than the other voices, are truly for people. They understand the value of putting relationships before opportunity on the priority list and have experienced moments where putting relationships first has brought benefits to others and peace in their own lives. Nurturers work from the assumption that everybody deserves to be heard and that people deserve the opportunity to bring their contribution. Without Nurturers there would be far fewer second chances and far less support and patience inside families or groups. Nurturers give people the chance to be who they are more than any other voice.

The Nurturer intuitively knows how the people inside teams and organizations are going to react to new ideas and strategies. They are like spiders at the center of a relational, emotional web that pick up the vibrations from much further out into the organization or network of friends. They are amazing sensors. They recognize that numbers are important, but regardless of how good the spreadsheet looks, the Nurturer wants to make sure the people are taken care of in the end. In this way, they function with a people-facing sixth sense in organizations, and they are normally spot-on when it comes to interpreting and anticipating peoples' motives and true intentions. Here is a perfect example of a Nurturer at work:

> Only six months into my law training at a mid-size practice, the senior partner (a Pioneer) asked me (a Nurturer) to take over the weekly support staff meetings—all the secretaries and receptionists. The partner was "tired of listening to their moaning," annoyed that they never seemed to have anything constructive to say and were constantly moving on. I began with some trepidation after these negative reports, and true, the first few meetings were basically lists of everything they thought was wrong with the firm. I concentrated on listening, changed a few basic things, which could have been done much earlier and would have made a big difference. I asked the staff to make suggestions more proactively and reasonably (they had just gotten used to being ignored). I began to get them to train each other in shortcuts and procedures, made the meetings more fun, brought homemade cake (honestly, that was probably the most successful weapon), arranged a Christmas party, and so on. Not rocket science, just basic nurturing skills. Support staff turnover fell from 75 percent the year before to 0. The law partner really didn't understand when I tried to explain how this had happened.

Nurturers are also incredibly pragmatic in their approach, asking questions like, "Has this really been thought through?" or "Is this the final plan?" Nurturers will ask the very practical, detailed questions because they feel responsible for the people on their team or in their life. Every change is going to affect someone and Nurturers tend to be the defenders of the values and feelings of others, sometimes to their own detriment. All Nurturers can point to times when, feeling responsible for someone who was sick or hurt or angry, they took the role of defending or helping with little care for their own benefit or health. In the end, it may have even led to the Nurturer receiving negative outcomes as a result of helping that person.

Nurturers are really gifted at discernment as well. By this we mean Nurturers have a knack for reading people and their true motives. Where other voices might charge the hill, the Nurturer is observing the other person and can usually sniff out any disconnection. Steve's wife, Helen, is a Nurturer. Here is how he describes her voice: "I've learned to value her judgment on people way more than I value my own. I'll say, 'So-and-so seemed really nice. What do you think?' and she's like, 'Mm.' That's Nurturer speak for, 'Stay well away. It's going to be a disaster,' because they just know. You can't hide from Nurturers. They know when people are genuine and when there is something not right. They intrinsically know who is for real and who's faking it. It's an invaluable gift to have in our marriage."

On a team, the Nurturer is the champion of relationships, relational harmony, and values. Those are the things Nurturers steward and the things for which they feel primarily responsible.

Nurturers inherently believe that how we choose to relate to one another in families, teams, and organizations is a higher priority than profit. It's not that profit is wrong or that they have an issue being part of profitable organizations, but Nurturers will champion values over profit if they come into conflict. How we choose to be with one another and how we choose to value each of the contributions people bring is much more important to them than to the other voices.

Because of these things, Nurturers will have a commitment to relational harmony before, during, and after difficult conversations. This means that Nurturers are thinking about how people will receive any words they share and preface them to make sure the person feels good before the conversation begins. Oftentimes during a conversation, they will interject positive words to ensure the person feels good or is comfortable. Immediately after a conversation, a Nurturer might go to the person with the calming words, "Are you okay?" or "Did you hear what I was trying to say?"

However difficult the conversation, however much dialogue happens on a team, however much somebody may have had their contribution critiqued or knocked down, the Nurturer inherently knows who needs a Starbucks coffee or a word of encouragement that says, "You know, I thought you really contributed today. I think they might have been a little bit harsh in the way that they tore your idea down. I want you to know at least I appreciated it."

Nurturers are like the oil inside the cogs of a complex engine. Wherever human beings interact with one another, there is the possibility and probability for eventual conflict. Nurturers, in their desire for harmony for the good of others, will function as mediators making sure some of the larger, maybe more combative voices, find a way to coexist in families, on teams, and in organizations.

And they tend to do it selflessly. They do it without any huge desire for credit and recognition, and they often are embarrassed when people push them forward and thank them for what they're doing: "No, no, it's fine. It's what I do." Very rarely will they gravitate toward the stage in a desire for public affirmation, but without the Nurturer voice present, any relational interactions are much less than they could be.

## What They Are Really Asking

Each voice is thinking something as it interacts and converses with the entire team. Here are the questions that Nurturers are really asking, usually quietly or silently:

1. "What are people going to be most upset about?" The Nurturer dislikes people getting frustrated or angry. Their emotional sensors are constantly aware of what others might become upset about, and they try to divert any negative energy before it begins.
2. "Could we change this to benefit everyone?" When Nurturers hear new ideas, they tend to ask the question as an advocate on behalf of the people who are going to be impacted by that change, and they wish others would communicate more effectively and thoughtfully.
3. "Is this a done deal? Are we really doing this?" Every Nurturer knows a moment in his life or his career where he started worrying about a particular directional strategy that turned out to be another voice simply talking out loud. The Nurturer became deeply concerned about the potential conflict before discovering that the idea was merely provisional and that there was no reason to worry at all.

Nurturers are very pragmatic and realistic people, because they usually feel responsible for the impact of a new decision or direction on people. They're always reminding themselves on behalf of the people they feel they represent: "If I'm going to be on the team, I'm not here primarily for me; I'm here for all the people who don't have input into this decision or don't have the ability to bring their contribution."

You won't always hear a Nurturer's question though, because they need a safe environment to know that when they share they're not going to be shot down immediately. And because they are always representing others, the Nurturer will often take information in without pressing the speaker for more details. A great example of this is a conversation that Helen and I (Steve) had one evening:

We were just about to go to bed and I casually mention, "Do you know, darling, I'm just getting worn out flying across the Atlantic from London to the United States all the time. I think at some stage we may need to move back to the United States as we continue to grow the GiANT business. Goodnight." I fall immediately to sleep, at peace with the world.

I wake up in the morning and Helen's there, exhausted. She has multiple lists open on the computer. She may not have actually been to sleep. I ask, as tenderly as I know how, "What's wrong? What are you doing?" She says, "I've been working out all the people we're going to have to talk to about leaving. How am I going to tell the grandparents that the children are moving 4,000 miles away?" She went on to ask, "Where are we going to live? When should we enroll them in schools? Who are all the people we need to say goodbye to and to thank for all they've done for us?" I respond, "I was only thinking out loud. I don't think it's practical at all. I think we're here for a long time."

I've learned from that experience (and many others like it) to duck at that point because that's when the missiles come.

Early on, the Nurturer should ask one of these questions, "Okay, before I start worrying about all the people who are going to be affected by this potential decision or change, is it a final decision? Do we really need to do this? What do you think the chances of it happening are?" There are learning opportunities for all of the voices, and for the Nurturer this is a worthy one. Because Nurturers are so committed to others, they can take on the stress of decisions before the decisions have actually been made, which causes everyone to become hypersensitive to a particular situation.

## What Is the Potential Negative Impact?

It is hard to find a negative impact for Nurturers because they're normally so amazingly nice, but immature Nurturers can often be so sensitive to everyone's needs that they become overly resistant to any change and cause others to walk on eggshells. Change, to a Nurturer, is generally not welcome, because of the amount of distress and disruption that it could cause others. And often the Nurturer feels unable to challenge the proposed direction, even if she knows it's wrong, because she doesn't want to deal with conflict or raise negative emotions.

Because Nurturers can see how future decisions will affect people, they will often have an opinion but not share it. Then, if the plans move forward and don't go well, the immature Nurturer will tend to say, "I knew this was going to happen!" And everyone else on the team gets frustrated because the Nurturer didn't share his opinion earlier when it could have made a huge difference.

Making money can also be seen as an impure motive for the immature Nurturer. They'll often claim this moral high ground, which annoys everyone else. The immature Nurturer will often throw in the gross generalization, "It's just about money for you, isn't it?" It's not usually true, but it's one of the immature Nurturer's default tendencies when he's feeling as if the values of the organization are being undermined in some way. This could lead an immature Nurturer to make accusations about the way money is being used and further alienate himself from other teammates.

And here's a quirk, particular to the Nurturer voice: Though everyone around them sees how competent and credible they are, Nurturers often struggle to believe that their contributions are valuable. (Recall Amy's story from earlier in the chapter.) They might not value the contribution they can make for a team or family. In fact, they tend to undervalue themselves and their contributions as they go on serving everyone else and dealing with others' problems. Believing in themselves and their voice is a key growth area for Nurturers.

Immature Nurturers can get so stuck wanting to help everyone else that they will often not move forward if faced with having to do so with any slight degree of uncertainty. Because they don't like conflict, the immature Nurturer also struggles to challenge others because it might negatively affect relational harmony. This can lead to passive-aggressive behavior because they feel they are defending people and values and not being listened to or affirmed. Nurturers can then become very frustrated with insensitive people, but are unable to challenge them appropriately out of fear or lack of experience at communicating anything that might be perceived as negative.

If you are a Nurturer, know that your views and opinions truly do matter. Every Nurturer asks, "Should I speak? Does anyone want to hear what I'm going to say? Should I even be here at this table?" Remember, people see you as a great resource; step into that role. It's time you started believing in your voice and its contribution.

The great thing about Nurturers is that you can tell them every single day that they're amazing and that you value their skills, and they'll never let that go to their heads. At their core they are truly humble leaders who want the very best for others on their team.

Foundational voice Nurturers, act as if you belong. Encourage people, raise their spirits, and become confident in how you are wired and what benefits you bring to the entire group. Learn to challenge the views of others on your team when you believe they're wrong. Please raise your voice. We all need to hear it.

## Insights for Nurturers

If you want to grow as a Nurturer, here are some key insights. Choose at least two comments below that might help you with your foundational voice in this next season:

1. When you speak you represent 43 percent of people. Your views and opinions truly matter! Share them more often.
2. People see you as a highly skilled professional. It's time you started to believe that!
3. People chose you to lead because they believe in you. Act knowing that you belong.
4. Learn to challenge the views of other voices on your team when you believe they are wrong.
5. Embrace change and help lead it. Don't be passive or function as a victim of change.
6. People trust your judgment and genuinely want to hear your opinion. Use that as a springboard for influence, and speak the truth in love.
7. When people challenge your views and opinions they are usually trying to help. It's not a personal attack.
8. Pioneers are not as insensitive and arrogant as you think. They just see the world differently than you do.

# 5
**◼**

# The Creative Voice

The Creative voice is so fascinating. Only 9 percent of the population has this voice as its foundational voice, which makes it rare and, quite often, misunderstood. The Creative thinks about the future constantly. In fact, Creatives are the champions of the big ideas of tomorrow, and they work diligently today to make the future take shape. They are the voice that creates the things that alter the future of organizations and teams.

The foundational Creative voice might be the CEO who is constantly innovating within the organization or the father who builds some amazing backyard games for the kids. Creatives are futurists, and while they can function in any role, they are overrepresented in the spheres of academia, design, technology, and not-for-profits.

Before we share specific details of this voice, let's listen to one of our CEO clients describe his Creative voice:

Learning the 5 Voices has been a game changer. Our two senior staff are both Nurturers, and it takes the two of them combined to corral my Creative voice and me. Before we learned about the 5 Voices, we would argue a lot about our future and what we were going to do. As a leader who has always respected his team, I would often bow to parliamentary procedure and get outvoted. I now understand my voice as a Creative and that I have to prepare my ideas more fully for others to understand them if there is any chance of them being implemented. Conversely, I know that if my ideas are not understood and accepted right away that it is not their fault; instead I need to regroup and organize my thoughts and try again.

The helpful reality is that our team understands me better as a Creative. They know if I'm bringing them something, it may be on the right path but not clear yet, so they need to help me "get it out" in a way that everyone else can get excited about, follow, and execute. We are the company's bookends, and if it makes sense to them and to me, then everyone else in between has hope!

The mature Creative has the ability to change the world, impact the growth of the organization, and dream up ideas or solutions the rest of us could never imagine on our own. The immature Creative, on the other hand, has the ability to frustrate the people around him and drive everyone else crazy in the process.

**What They Are Thinking**

Just like the Nurturer, Creatives come to the table with certain unspoken assumptions running in the background of their minds that shape how they process, respond, and behave. Never satisfied with the status quo, and regardless of how good something is, foundational voice Creatives are always thinking, "I'm sure we could make it better."

The word "can't" is not part of a Creative's vocabulary, either. If they see a compelling vision of the future that they're drawn to, you'll hear them say, "We will find a way," when they run into obstacles. There's no end to the ingenuity of the Creative voice. And as such, they tend to have strong perfectionist tendencies. Because their vision of the future is so exciting, Creatives will fight for the ideal in their minds until they see it become reality.

Creatives also presume, most often based on their life experiences, that people have difficulty fully understanding what it is they are trying to say. Here's how this plays out: Paul, a graphic designer for an ad agency, has a vision for a branding campaign his company wants to pitch. He can visualize the logo, the magazine ads, all of it in its entirety, and he's very excited by what he sees coming together in his mind. He shares his vision with his creative director and the lead on the sales team and gets a flat response, barely a reaction. He goes back to the drawing board, literally, to try again, but isn't sure there's any point, so he moves on to another project. A month later, sitting in a meeting, Paul listens to a colleague share nearly the same idea, to which the creative director says, "Brilliant. Let's do that." Confounded and angry, Paul vents to the sales lead sitting next to him, "But I said that a month ago! Why didn't anyone listen?" The sales lead says, "What you said sounded nothing like that." Exasperated, Paul internally questions his value, thinking to himself, "I'm not sure why I bother to show up some days."

For any foundational voice Creative reading this, you're likely nodding your head thinking of your own similar experiences. What most people miss, and what we've learned, is that Creatives communicate and function best when they truly know that their contributions are valued and appreciated. Because they struggle to clearly articulate their ideas at first, they often get shot down, which means they eventually shut down. Given this, other unspoken questions include: "Is this a safe environment? Are my ideas and opinions valued? Are the others I'm with for me? Are they encouraging me to bring my voice, willing to ask clarifying questions to understand fully what it is I'm trying to say?" Knowing these truths, let's explore what Creatives at their best can do.

## What They Bring at Their Best

Of all the foundational voices, Creatives have the ability to see the future first. They are the people who are always scanning the horizon for new ideas, new trends, and new technologies coming our way. They see opportunities, as well as threats, long before the other voices, because they spend so much of their internal, creative thinking time focused on the future.

We can only imagine the tension that many Creatives feel as a result of this future-focused orientation. They see what's coming, for better or worse. The Creative voice has the most skilled early warning radar system, particularly when a team, organization, or family is beginning to become inauthentic in the way it functions. Most Creatives are very principled people who operate with a high degree of integrity and authenticity and always seek to align what they care about and say with what they actually do.

Creatives also have an early warning radar system and can see when there's danger ahead, particularly when the organization or the team is in danger of compromising its values.

Healthy Creatives working on an appreciative and mature team can be free to be the advance guard, going ahead of the rest to see if the way is safe or not. Their sniff test, so to speak, can provide indispensable information in much the same way canaries were used in coal mines long ago. Sensitive to carbon monoxide, the birds would accompany miners into the unventilated shafts. If their singing stopped, that was the signal for the miners that the carbon monoxide levels were becoming dangerous.

Because other voices aren't equipped to see so far out on the horizon and recognize when something isn't right, Creatives are a tremendous resource for groups and teams. They see what the rest of us miss.

Brilliant conceptual architects, Creatives think outside the box more than any of the other foundational voices. They are often the ones bringing a revolutionary insight or an innovative solution to a complex problem. Creatives tend to think in ways that are least aligned with the common understanding or what the majority is thinking, which can make communicating their ideas a challenge.

For the Creative, exploring the future is far more exciting than maintaining the present, which is already here. Creatives are purists at heart. They are idealists with a strong sense of social justice, they want to ensure that the organization they work for is making a difference for its people and contributing to the well-being of the local community. That's an incredible asset to any team, organization, or group of people.

Lastly, Creatives drive innovation and promote growth and improvement, even when others begin to settle: "But we could do this better," they'll say. "Good enough" is never good enough for the Creative voice at its best. When kept in check, this attribute can help teams strive to reach beyond where the bar is set, but in instances where Creatives lack awareness or are undisciplined, their perfectionist tendencies can be damaging.

## What They Are Really Asking

Most Creatives are quieter characters. You'll typically find them sitting and listening for a period of time, perhaps writing or journaling, as some of the other louder voices share their ideas with bravado and vigor. In these moments, Creatives are contemplating, running the ideas through their filters and analyzing the validity of the ideas being presented. The question they are asking is, "So what? How does this actually help us achieve the vision of the future that we're most excited about?" Discovering the answer will usually involve testing the idea with someone else to ensure values are not going to be compromised in a way that might be regretted later.

When called on to share, they are also asking internally, "Are you ready to listen to what I need to share?" And when Creatives speak, it's because they actually have something to share; they do not typically waste words. If they don't have anything to share they won't speak, which is not true for some of the other voices! But they need to know that others around them are ready to listen and truly want to help them communicate effectively.

Lastly, Creatives ask, "Why are we limiting ourselves?" Constantly pushing the envelope and running toward the frontier, they need to know that they have the freedom to dream big and innovate and that you are with them and for them in the process.

So, if Nurturers are the custodians of relationships, relational value, harmony, and integrity, Creatives are champions of the future. They love the future and will fight for it, and function best when they are positioned to be the social conscience of an organization they believe in.

## What Is the Potential Negative Impact?

For all its positive contributions, every voice can have a negative impact as well. The immature Creative can cause a lot of damage. Their desire to always do better and their perfectionist tendencies about the ideal vision of the future can often wear people out. When nearly everyone else is ready to party and celebrate a win or move on to another project, the Creative can throw cold water on the party by pointing out how something could be improved or done better, rather than simply celebrating the success. Rather than seeing the 90 percent accomplished, they hyper-focus on the 10 percent that's incomplete or not up to their high standards, which can, at best, be draining to those in their circle and divisive at worst. For the hospital administrator who chastises the medical team for incomplete paperwork on the heels of a 10-hour surgery that saved a life, or the parent who looks at the report card and only criticizes the C rather than celebrating the As and Bs, it shouldn't be a surprise when nurses complain of feeling undervalued or quit, or when children

> *Rather than seeing the 90 percent accomplished, Creatives can hyper-focus on the 10 percent that's incomplete.*

become distant or apathetic. In these examples, the ill will from those on the receiving end of the Creative's critique reflects this lack of awareness.

Idealism, another potential speed bump, will often trump pragmatism for the immature Creative and can lead to a sense of paralysis. Unless Creatives can visualize how something can be done and become passionate about that vision, they find it very hard to start the project. Do you want to help a Creative get unstuck? The best way is to have that individual show you what he has to date and then tell him that you are going to commit to helping him get his big idea down on paper. If Creatives don't see progress, they will often delay working on a project or just stop entirely and move on to something else. If you can catch a glimpse of what they are really trying to do and show them you believe in it, then you can help pull the idea out of them.

Creatives can perfectly envision what they want to achieve. However, they can get quite finicky if they feel that their project is not receiving enough support. This hypersensitivity about their ideal vision can frustrate everyone involved. The Creative is thinking, "Why would we do something when it isn't going to be as good as I would wish it to be?" Some of you are smiling because you know this is you, while others of you are grimacing, as you have had to deal with this person recently.

Lastly, immature Creatives often tend to ignore financial constraints and practical realities. This can cause difficulties for those around them who tend to be a bit more practical and pragmatic. Because Creatives see the future as concrete, they are willing to step forward in pursuing it while ignoring seeming barriers (like costs), all the while trusting that their sixth-sense intuitiveness and their vision of the future as such a 'lock' that those things will be overcome in due time. If they are not careful, immature Creatives can lose influence, and, as a result, they can undermine the opportunity to reach the dream they have in their heads.

## How to Help the Creative

Creatives need people on the other side of them to actually say, "We want to hear your ideas and we want to help you get there." Creatives want help to pull off the big dreams in their heads, but they don't want intrusion or someone trying to control the process. They want the freedom to do what it is they have in their minds, but they also want others to value them in the process. If you will take the time to ask the right questions and have the patience to hear what it is they are really trying to say, then what comes out eventually will be pure gold. Creatives rarely say anything coherent the first time even though in their minds they think they have! They need to have others ask clarifying questions to mine the gold buried within. Here is how LV Hanson, a Creative from Huntington Beach, California, tells it in his own words:

> My personal capacity to influence my team and my leaders has grown significantly since learning and applying the genius of the 5 Voices. As a Creative, I find that my ideas and dreams are often communicated too quickly and passionately, leaving me wishing I had never opened my mouth in the first place. I can be quick to fire with what I'm convinced is a great idea, but because I don't take time to vet it or collaborate with key influencers, I can fall victim to what I call the diminishing return of passion. At the peak of my excitement and passionate vision casting, I must be ready to pass the baton to key Nurturers and Guardians who can take my ideas to new heights, which assumes I have already built a bridge to them. My tendency has been to allow my excitement and passion to peak and when nobody responds, I turn up the excitement and passion ultimately leading to my own demise—it quickly turns into a free fall of diminishing return. . . . The very thing that brought me to a significant peak is the very thing that erodes it. I can start something special, but my ability to win lies in my ability to patiently, intentionally, and strategically communicate and collaborate with key connectors.

As mentioned earlier, Creatives are a rare voice with only 9 percent of people identifying Creative as their foundational voice. If you help them they can truly positively impact those around them. However, it will take patience and commitment and firm resolve to pull out the big ideas that need to be heard.

If you are a Creative, choose two statements that you believe will help you improve your voice and change your world.

1. Learn to celebrate the wins even if they weren't quite as perfect as you hoped.
2. When members of your team critique your vision and ask for the details, they are genuinely trying to help you.
3. Don't play safe; give yourself permission to think outside the box and dream.
4. It's okay to be wrong sometimes, it comes with the territory of creativity and imagination.
5. What you see as an imminent opportunity or threat may actually be further away than you think.
6. Financial realities are important; good enough may have to be good enough sometimes.
7. People are not deliberately ignoring your ideas; it's simply hard to truly hear a Creative.
8. You don't have to prove your worth to teammates, relax and trust in the unique contribution you bring.

# 6

## The Guardian Voice

The Guardian. What an incredibly valuable foundational voice and yet, the one that is often the least appreciated of the five. Guardians do what their name implies: they guard, protect, and defend. Yet Guardians are often misunderstood because they can be viewed as a wet blanket on the ideas of the futurists and the dreamers. They are wired to question change and have an innate ability to understand why something won't work, which can cause them to appear negative. The reality, though, is that Guardians are vital to the health of teams and groups: They keep companies afloat, keep families on the right track, and are the engines that help make great ideas actually happen in real life.

Guardians comprise 30 percent of the population, and 70 percent of them are men. Interestingly, this is the direct opposite of the Nurturer where 70 percent are female.

Guardians are by nature conservative leaders; when they pioneer they do so based on years of expertise and unconscious competence in their chosen field. They are rock-like characters who provide an incredible sense of security, stability, and consistency for those they lead. They champion discipline, systems, and infrastructure and have a right and wrong filter that helps keep order. When you begin to understand and value the contribution of the foundational voice Guardian, your team productivity will go to a new level. Without Guardians, companies would run out of money, teams would go adrift into random idea land, and things simply wouldn't get finished.

## What They Are Thinking

Some characters, like the foundational voice Creative, love exploring the future of what could be and what has never been done before. Guardians, however, are present-oriented and typically respond with facts about reality rather than speculation. They think logically and have consistent questions in their mind that can be churned out like machine gun fire. They need proof before they move forward and are believers in the adage, "If it isn't broken, why fix it?" They are intent on understanding why change is really necessary and will insist on being convinced before buying into whatever other voices propose. Guardians are always thinking: "Convince me that change is really necessary." They need it to make logical sense before saying yes to a major change.

And, having been disappointed at some point by a persuasive Connector or Pioneer whose plans didn't materialize, they also operate under the assumption that if it looks too good to be true, it probably is. Every Guardian remembers the one time in their life when they suspended their rational, critical, logical judgment and bought a timeshare or invested in something that they didn't really understand or believe, but because everyone else was so for it they went ahead and said yes. After this event they vowed, "I will never, ever, ever, ever again do anything if it looks too good to be true without doing my due diligence."

If Guardians had time or energy to share their thoughts, they would say to all the other voices, "For goodness sake, if you would only realize I'm not here to make your life miserable or pour cold water on all of your great ideas for changing the world. What I'm trying to bring is my contribution, which actually is essential even though it's not necessarily going to be popular. I am simply trying to make sure we don't waste time and money when we don't need to."

The foundational voice Guardian frequently feels the frustration of his contribution being marginalized or seen as the negative, critical, glass-half-empty type of person. That's not who they are but it's how they believe others often see them.

Another unspoken thought is that "people would be astonished if they knew how smart I truly am." Their internal question to any pushback is, "do you really not know how helpful and valuable my contribution is to this discussion? I know a lot about a lot of things that could help you."

Every Guardian deals with the frustration of having to listen to someone's lengthy so-called brilliant idea or proposal, usually with some kind of cost involved, without being able to instantly address all the reasons why it is unlikely to work. The Guardian then begins to share the logical, rational, analytical bullets explaining why the idea is likely to fail, which is not usually received in the best light. This tends to lead to the branding of the Guardian as a wet blanket or a killjoy. The

unspoken thought is really this: "I wish people would understand that I'm not trying to make everyone miserable and
annoyed. I'm just trying to play my role, and I'm trying to
make sure we don't squander resources, talent, and money
when we don't need to."

## What They Bring at Their Best

At their best, foundational voice Guardians bring a relentless
commitment to ask the difficult questions. Regardless of how
exciting a charismatic leader's idea may sound, the Guardian
always takes on the responsibility to understand the forensic
detail and determine how (and if!) it is actually going to work.
They will keep asking questions that are difficult, tough, and
even awkward until they either get satisfactory answers or
figure it out for themselves. And we need them to keep asking.
That is their job. They lean into difficult topics or situations
and embrace challenge instead of running away or trying to
please everyone involved. Guardians tend to be laser-focused
on being precise, diligent, consistent, and thorough and they
refuse to give up. Imagine the possibilities when other voices
begin to value these qualities and see them as strengths rather
than viewing them in a negative light.

Even more, at their best, Guardians have an unbelievable
capacity to deliver on time and on budget once the vision and
objectives have been agreed upon. Of all the voices, Guardians
are the most committed to delivering on the promises they
have made. If you look a Guardian in the eye and ask, "Have
you got all the details you need? Do you know what the
success criteria are?" and if they say yes and believe in the
project, you can be assured that they would rather die than fail
to deliver on what they have committed to do. As a deadline

nears, Guardians will become ever more focused on finishing so as not to let the team down or fail to deliver what they have committed to. Relational niceties such as sleep, meals, and everything else fall second to meeting the deadline or goal they committed to. It is a huge asset for any team to know that someone, once they've committed, will carry the ball and deliver it on time and on budget. Guardians also have the capacity to detach personal sentiment when they have to make tough decisions. (Note: There can be negative consequences to such focus, and we will study what those are just ahead.)

In the end, making the right decision on behalf of the whole team and the organization is more important to a Guardian than an individual's personal feelings. It may be their spouse, it may be their brother, it may be their best friend, but if they think the other person is wrong, they will challenge him, because the truth and making the right decision on behalf of the greater good of the organization, family, or group is more important than relational niceties with the people in front of them.

At their best, Guardians protect what is already working. Guardians are aware of all of the people who have made sacrifices to get the team and the organization to where they are today. They normally don't mind going after new things and new opportunities, but they want to make sure that in the process the organization won't lose what it has already won.

So, if Nurturers are champions of relationships, values, and relational harmony, and Creatives are champions of the future and of the social conscience, Guardians are champions of tradition and resources; they feel an innate responsibility for how money, time, and energy are spent. Where money is concerned, though they may not be the owner of the business, they carry a level of commitment and discipline for spending and stewarding that is unparalleled and treat every dollar spent as if it were their own. It goes without saying how necessary this is for families, teams, and organizations.

Listen to the breakthrough that happened when Brandon Hutchins, a Guardian from Marietta, Georgia, truly understood the power of his voice:

Learning the 5 Voices language and realizing that I was a foundational voice Guardian has helped give me more confidence to be how God designed me to be. I felt like I was naturally compelled to protect people and organizations from making bad/uninformed decisions by asking difficult questions and requiring additional details. Over time I've felt a heaviness that has come with my Guardian voice, because of how momentum-killing questioning can be to groups. As I've learned the language, it's given me more freedom to be present and be the best possible version of a mature Guardian. Specifically, I've learned to help others to engage me as a Guardian to help them guard what is most important to them through accountability. I've also learned to insert other's feelings and values as a part of my question filter to accompany other details like cost, schedule, and capacity.

I have learned that my wife is a Nurturer/Connector, and I can see the way she naturally speaks these voices in our family and with our friends. Many times, she needs me to turn off the critical/question-oriented Guardian voice so she can provisionally talk through plans and ideas. While she very much appreciates the safe way in which my Guardian voice communicates and manages our family, most times she is not looking for me to solve her problems with questions or ideas.

As I am becoming more confident and mature in who I am, I am much more appreciative of others and the voices they bring. I can now help them to bring their best to the table and to be aware of the negatives that commonly come with their natural voice.

That is a great picture of a mature Guardian bringing his best to his team and family. The Guardian also believes in guarding what already has been working brilliantly. They will look at all the things that have been hard won—all the money, all the resources, all the learning—and when people are trying to do new things the Guardian is always the one who will ask, "Are we in danger of throwing the baby out with the bathwater?" It's important to recognize that while Guardians can also enjoy being able to shape the future vision and direction, they bring the necessary caution: "Let's not squander or lose all the ground that has been claimed, all the breakthroughs that have happened."

Lastly, Guardians know the person who sat in your seat 20 years ago. They will know the person who made the personal sacrifice that allows you to have capital to invest right now. They know who did what to set the organization or team up for success. That is what Guardians do. They'll know the people upon whose shoulders the team is now building, and they will always, always seek to honor their memory.

## What They Are Really Asking

Because Guardians love to ask questions that keep the organization or family safe and moving forward, here is a list of questions they are really asking:

- Is it really worth the risk and investment?
- What happens if it isn't quite as good as we think it is?
- What's our worst-case scenario?
- You're projecting these revenue numbers, but if we only get 30 percent of it, what's the consequence?

- Have we really done our due diligence before we commit time, money, and resources to a particular project?
- Can we test the hypothesis before we go all in?

Again, these questions are meant to help people. The more mature the foundational Guardian voice, the easier this is to understand.

Years ago, Jeremie worked with a company board member who was ruthless on numbers. Here's how he learned to value the Guardian voice: "In all of our advances and big ideas, I knew that by the time our board meeting came around I'd better have all our contingencies in place, from what would happen if a terrorist attack occurred to how we were going to manage fixed costs if our events went flat or we missed our projections. The team would try to outthink him by planning answers to any possible questions he might ask. In the end, though, there was always a particular question that would get right to the issue that the group of Connectors, Creatives, and Pioneers had missed. His questions were helpful, even if at times they felt like attacks."

Guardians are usually advocates of pilot programs. They like to pilot things in one area of the business where it can be analyzed so the kinks can be worked out before rolling it out to the rest of the business. While other foundational Voices can find running a pilot frustrating and time consuming, the Guardians understand the minutia required and work to set a realistic pace where people, resources, and money are well stewarded and not squandered.

Where personal relationships are concerned, the Guardian is asking, "Am I at risk of being taken advantage of?" Most Guardians have a horror story from their past where a gifted, charismatic communicator sold them something for which they weren't quite sure they had all the details. That is one of the primary reasons they ask their logical questions.

## What Is the Potential Negative Impact?

Every voice has a positive and negative aspect. If the person is mature, the voice will tend to be more positive. Conversely, if a person is immature then we will more often see the negative impact of that voice. Immature Guardians can often find it difficult to compromise when they have a strongly held opinion. The whole team can be in agreement, but immature Guardians still can't see it. They'll dig in their heels and hold their position, refusing to let go out of a relentless stubbornness, just like a dog with a bone.

The desire for truth and for the right decision will often override their personal sentiment for people as well. If they are not careful, they can appear overly critical and harsh when sharing their views, making others feel attacked. Foundational voice Guardians always have to be aware of these tendencies. Even though their desire for truth and making the right decision is noble, it's imperative that they remember there are people on the other end of that critique and challenge, many of whom, as we'll see later, don't wear the same body armor that the average Guardian does. Dave Loeffel, from Atlanta, Georgia, says it best:

> As a Guardian, it is not my first instinct to appreciate the impact of decisions (or the decision-making process itself) on the way people feel. Understanding this helps me guard my expressions and words to ensure that people know I am open to feedback and actually want it, and motivates me to ask for feedback from Nurturers about the emotional impact of decisions. When I am trying to do something organizationally, I filter my communications through Nurturers before going live with any big new ideas.

This is a great example of a mature Guardian under-standing the potential negative consequences of his voice and how to value the contribution of others and communicate more effectively inside his team.

The immature Guardian can often wear everyone out by actually insisting, "Unless I can see it we're not going anywhere." Or, they can ask so many questions that they eventually undermine their own authority and respect because people begin to work around them to get things accomplished.

Oftentimes their desire to determine what is logical and correct and true can sound like interrogation to other people. It is normally Guardians' tone and lack of tact that limit their influence. They then can become overly critical and at times insensitive to the relational needs of those they are engaging with. Guardians can be right and wrong at the same time!

The opposite can be true with a mature, respectful Guardian. Observe how a Guardian thinks. Marina Ulinuic from Romania tells her story here:

> I am very structured and put a lot of pressure on myself to achieve. I used to find it incredibly difficult to work with people who were impractical dreamers who, as I saw it, were not organized or reliable. As deadlines approached I would express my frustrations and it would often lead to conflict and relational tension. When I discovered the 5 Voices, I finally realized *why* this conflict happened. For a foundational voice Guardian it's such a relief to understand the *why* behind our team dynamics. I have taken the time to learn and understand what each voice brings at its best, and I now know what it feels like to be on the other side of a Guardian critique! My team now understands me and actively encourages me to ask the difficult questions."

What you begin to find is each foundational voice has its nemesis voice. Those of you who are foundational voice Creatives love exploring the future and know that if the vision is compelling you will figure out the details as you go. On the other hand, Guardians need to know the destination and the clear incremental steps of how the team will get there before they will leave the comfort of their present reality. The Guardian is the nemesis voice of the Creative; the two often miss each other!

Remember, we speak all of the voices, but we have one as our primary, foundational voice through which each of the others is filtered and heard. In later chapters we will help you confirm your voice order to understand the complexity of who you are from the lens of nature, nurture, and choice.

In the meantime, here are some points to consider as you grow in effectiveness and maturity as a Guardian. Choose two that you can work on right now and begin implementing into your life:

1. How you communicate is important (volume and sensitivity). It's possible for you to be right and wrong at the same time. Remember to manage your tone and tact. Look to healthy Nurturers if you need examples to imitate.
2. Learn to value the future-orientated voices; they drive innovation and progress.
3. Sometimes goalposts move on projects and it's not anyone's fault.
4. Learning to compromise is a healthy part of team life.
5. Be careful: constantly driving yourself and your team will eventually lead to burnout and resentment.
6. Take time to invest in your key relationships today; you are not defined by task achievement alone.

7. Your team knows you are competent. Do they know that you care?
8. Networking events and social media platforms are not a waste of time. Invest in them.

# 7

# The Connector Voice

Ah, the Connector. Everyone likes Connectors, or so they hope. This is the voice that makes meetings fun and appears to be the life of the party. They know how to carry a room and can transition from one conversation to the next with relative ease. Give a Connector a problem or an idea, and if he doesn't already have the resources or relationships to meet the need, he will find someone who does. Foundational voice Connectors take great pride in making things happen for other people and maintain a high volume of friendships. Affable characters, healthy Connectors are easy to like. But when lacking self-awareness, Connectors can be perceived as super-ficial pleasers and frustrate others with their constant bouncing from one thing to the next, like the famed Tigger character in *Winnie the Pooh*.

The Connector is the voice that doesn't seem to get tired or worn out by people or new ideas. Connectors thrive on spinning plates and making connections, as they seem to effortlessly remember details about what other people are working on and what they might need.

## What They Are Thinking

Foundational voice Connectors think very differently than Guardians do. They are often thinking about tomorrow and how their connections can play together on projects or initiatives.

"If I love it, everyone's going to love it!" That's the unspoken assumption for most Connectors. It doesn't matter if it is a movie or a restaurant or a business colleague they want to introduce you to, whatever Connectors are into they are going to use all their persuasive abilities to convince you that you should be, too. And chances are, they will!

Connectors value collaboration. It's one thing for them to be excited about a new opportunity, but what they really want is everyone else on the team to be as excited as they are, too. It's never quite as much fun for the Connector if there are four people who are really for something and two against it; Connectors want everyone to be all in. Collaboration, therefore, as an unspoken assumption sounds like this question: "We're all in this together; how do we all win together?"

Connectors, as their name implies, are always making connections for people. As they listen to others, they're always thinking, "Whatever we need, I can get it. I have a source." Connectors are unbelievable at knowing who has what and who needs this or that. They have a knack for finding jobs for people and for generating ideas, and they always have advice to offer others. Therefore, their common question is, "Who do I know who can do this or that?"

Because most Connectors are incredibly relational people who appear ultimately altruistic in the way they lavish their connections and opportunities, they usually expect some measure of appreciation or acknowledgment for the connections they've made or the benefits they have brought. They want recognition. It's that sort of fame that makes the Connector's world go round.

Every Connector can tell stories of everyday interactions on airplanes or having coffee when they met someone for the first time and built a new friendship. One trip to Starbucks later, and they have three new friends "you just have to meet!" Everyone else wonders at this unceasing three-ring circus, but for the Connector who is always connecting people and ideas, it's just a natural by-product of what they expect each day to be.

## What They Bring at Their Best

At their best, what do Connectors bring to the table? Connectors, of all the voices, have the greatest capacity to maintain the largest number of relationships. It's incredible how many friends the average Connector actually has. They'll introduce every single person to you like this: "I want you to meet Melissa; she's a dear friend of mine." Some of the other voices will ask, "How can anybody have that many close friends?" Connector relationships have no half-life; there is no decay over time. With Connectors, whatever the quality of the relationship was the last time you saw them is exactly where they'll reconnect with you. They may not have seen you since kindergarten, but if you were close then, they will just pick up from that period of time. It's amazing. Foundational voice Connectors have this incredible, relational vortex that sucks people into their world in a way that makes the other person feel cared for, valued, and known. This is the world of a Connector.

Connectors know how to bring people together with their aspirations. They have the innate ability to listen to people and their goals and take steps to help them accomplish the things that they want to see happen. Oftentimes, Connectors will spend

*Connectors know how to connect* more time helping others
*people and their aspirations.* than helping themselves, which can be frustrating to the spouse of a Connector. A Connector's strength can also be a weakness.

They are the most incredible salespeople because they don't believe themselves to be salespeople. They are never selling, they are just being themselves: passionate problem solvers who connect people to resources with an enthusiasm that is infectious and draws people in. When it comes to marketing, messaging, and the external communication of ideas, the Connector voice is utterly invaluable because they know what connects with peoples' aspirations. Gifted with the ability to intuit how people are feeling about a topic and excellent at reading signals, they inherently know how to pitch ideas with creative ingenuity. And because they're usually people of enormous integrity, they won't sell things they don't believe in.

For Connectors, life is just a huge adventure to be shared with as many people over as many exciting possibilities and opportunities as possible. It's very hard to keep a Connector down for long because there's always something new to be excited about. They're very good at scouting out collaborative partnerships beyond the immediate world of where their business is right now, and they have the patience to connect with people and plant seeds for future benefit.

Listen to Connector Jay Sampson from Shawnee, Oklahoma, share what he has learned by going through the 5 Voices training:

> As a Connector, I have come to realize that there are some things that I do that add tremendous value in a team environment. Because I am not hard to inspire and love working with teams on ideas, I can often see how great things could be in the future. Particularly when I am working with a team that I truly believe in, my juices get flowing thinking of how these great people can be even greater with the addition of key connections that I have.
>
> I truly believe that there is nothing that can't be accomplished with the right team of people. I often dream big and then think about who needs to be pulled in to make that happen. My value to the team is that I become the indispensable "glue guy" who makes everyone and everything stick. The Connector thrives on standing back after an accomplishment by the team knowing that he or she was connected to everyone in the process.

The most mature Connectors are givers and are for others as much as they're for themselves when they are at their best. They genuinely love giving away what it is they have for the sheer joy of seeing more people being able to share in the experience.

Amazing storytellers, Connectors are persuasive and inspirational communicators who are very good at drawing people in. And you'll find that when they're selling you something, they always go for your heart first with a compelling human-interest story about someone whose life has been transformed or something that is personal.

The Connector's glass is always at least half full. They are generally very positive people who see limitless opportunities ahead of them. Because of this they constantly look for the chance to interact with other people, share their stories, hear what other people are up to, and add value to others as much as they can. In the end, if they believe in what they are promoting then it's not a problem selling it, because they want the people they're sharing it with to experience all the wonderfully positive things that they themselves have experienced. It's never to meet a target. That's the reason why they're so good at it. Connectors would rather live with less money than feel that they were inauthentic or that they somehow misrepresented something to people.

## What They're Really Asking

Each voice always draws on an internal list of questions to gather information to make decisions, which they may not actually verbalize. Here's what frames any conversation or decision-making process for the foundational voice Connector:

- How are we going to connect this incredible opportunity to the maximum number of people?
- How will this idea connect to help others inside or outside of the company?
- How do we make sure the most people get a benefit from it?
- You really can't see it?

Once they've relayed an idea they are passionate about with all their charm and persuasive tactics, most Connectors find it quite unbelievable when someone else isn't as excited about it as they are or doesn't even understand it. It's utterly incomprehensible that something that is so obvious to them is not obvious to the rest of the world. Hardwired to want everyone to be all in, the persistent Connector will pivot and try a new approach, determined to get buy-in from everyone. In the process, you'll commonly hear Connectors ask, "Is everyone still with me?" Or, "Are we good? Are we all on the same page? Everyone good?" Because it's much more fun for the Connector when we're all moving forward together toward what it is we're trying to achieve rather than doing it alone. Connectors don't like being consistently alone. And knowing this, you can probably already see how the nemesis voice for Connectors might be Guardians, with their questions that might make the Connector feel as though they are not collaborating.

## What Is the Potential Negative Impact?

Connectors love to be loved and, therefore, often tend to be people pleasers if they're not careful. And what they'll often do, without realizing it, is sell things slightly differently to different people to improve their chance of getting 100 percent buy-in. You'll often find people will come together saying, "Hang on, what you were sold sounds slightly different than what I was sold." They feel somehow deceived when a Connector, lacking awareness, manipulates a sales pitch. This is not at all the intention of the Connector, though; it's merely a misguided attempt to persuade everyone to go all in.

The immature Connector is also often guilty of creating a boomerang effect by turning everything back around to focus on himself. When someone shares a story, the Connector will say, "That reminds of the time when I . . ." This lack of self-awareness can wear others out and, unbeknownst to the Connector, can undermine his influence.

Another negative tendency of immature Connectors is taking critiques of their ideas too personally. Connectors put every part of themselves into the ideas they bring to the table. Wisdom for Connectors is learning to separate their emotions from their ideas and learning to see rejection of an idea not as a personal failure or a critique of their character. An immature Connector will hear someone say, "That's really great you shared that with us, but we don't think this is the right time to proceed," as a personal attack. Immature Connectors will then continue to sell the idea, only louder, until they realize their strategy isn't working. This is when the passive aggressive behavior begins, and the immature Connector will withdraw and become irrational in his view of the relationship, which has now been damaged. In the end, for the immature Connector, rejection of an idea feels like a questioning of his own value and the validity of his integrity because, "I wouldn't be selling it if it wasn't true. I wouldn't be bringing it to you if it wasn't actually what we need."

If they aren't careful, immature Connectors can often be accused of being slightly manipulative with information and almost appear to be playing people to get them to do what they want them to. They will share their ideas with incredible passion, tell personal stories designed to make everyone cry, and at times that can be perceived as inauthentic.

Here is how Connector Don Peslis from Oklahoma City, Oklahoma, illustrates his realities:

5 Voices would have saved me countless days of frustration, misunderstanding, and basic wailing and gnashing of teeth. As a young, energized Connector/Creative leader, I was fully convinced that the vision, idea, and ultimate plans that I was proposing were the best options. Then came along

those annoying, bothersome, and probing questions offered up by people who I now know to be Guardians and Nurturers. Did they not understand that we were about to change the world? Looking back I never truly listened to anything they said. I smiled politely at their words of caution but felt they were being overcautious and moved ahead anyway. I reflect now on just how much time, money, and effort would have been saved if I'd been able to truly hear the contribution of all 5 Voices then. I now understand the importance of preparation, due diligence, and pilot projects.

The foundational voice Connector, along with the Pioneer and Creative are the future-oriented voices, while the Nurturer and Guardian tend to be the present-minded voices. Just like the name suggests, the Connector has the ability to connect the future to the present and vice versa and, thus, plays a vital role on every team.

Only 11 percent of the population speaks Connector as their foundational voice. While they are future-oriented, they have an understanding of where other people are coming from, which makes them great translators for those inside and outside the team or organization.

Maturity is the key to properly leveraging the Connector voice. The only problem is that maturity usually comes from being challenged, which can feel like failure or rejection at times, especially if it comes from someone who isn't actively for the Connector.

Here are ways that a foundational voice Connector can be challenged to grow. Choose two that you believe will help you improve your Connector voice the most.

1. Remember, when people reject your idea, it's not as personal as it sometimes feels.

2. Hinting at your frustrations with teammates does not guarantee anyone has truly heard you. Be direct in your feedback. Ask specific questions that open the door for action.

3. People will critique your ideas. Learn to avoid the knee-jerk reaction of becoming overly defensive.

4. It's okay to be you! When you believe something passionately, never be afraid to share it.

5. Encourage the team to critique your ideas, and remember the team will make them better.

6. Avoid oversharing, especially when you are emotionally frustrated.

7. Be intentional—take time to think through how you can create a culture where other voices can bring their best.

8. Be patient with those whose due diligence process is rigorous, painful, and time consuming.

# 8 | ◼ The Pioneer Voice

The Pioneer voice touches the red zone on the decibel level, not necessarily because of its volume but because of the force with which Pioneers communicate their opinions. They are powerful characters whose logic and rationality make them very hard to argue with. They enjoy the challenge of leadership and readily accept the responsibility that goes with it. The Pioneer is a future-oriented voice, with the ability to coordinate resources and people to turn big ideas into accomplishments. At their best, Pioneers galvanize and inspire teams to achieve incredible things, but at their worst they can divide people and destroy things.

## What They Are Thinking

Pioneers are constantly thinking, and this is what makes them so valuable. Most of their thinking is focused on strategic problem solving and how they are going to achieve the biggest possible win!

For a foundational voice Pioneer, visioning the future is always the highest priority. They have immense self-belief and inherently believe that anything is possible. To challenge the competency of a Pioneer is the equivalent of waving a red flag in front of the proverbial bull. When someone tells a Pioneer that they can't do something, the reply is usually, "Who says we can't? Watch and I'll show you." The Pioneer often thinks, "If we're going to do it, let's go big or go home." The vision of a Pioneer is rarely ever anything short of true global domination, and the monologue about the next big idea sounds something like this: "We might pilot it locally. We might try it in the city. Then we go regional. Then we can go national. Then we go continental. Then we go global. Then we go intergalactic, and eventually we'll open our French bakery (or whatever the big idea is) on Pluto." Once the vision has been locked in, Pioneers work to assemble the highest capacity team and start building scalable infrastructure. Pioneers are highly competitive characters and as leaders they invariably assume, "If you're around my table you're in." They enjoy winning and assume that all of their team will give everything to achieve the agreed upon objective. When foundational voice Pioneers are mature and intentional they make sure all of the other voices in the group are heard and valued. Their self-assured confidence is infectious and other voices are able to bring their best, safe in the knowledge that the Pioneer is happy to take on the ultimate responsibility for success.

**What They Bring at Their Best**

At their best, Pioneers bring the greatest capacity of all the voices to align people, systems, and resources to deliver long-term complex visions. Pioneers are by nature militaristic. They like to fight and they hate to lose. They love strategy and will spend many hours assessing how best to deploy their resources on the battlefield. For most this would constitute work, but for foundational voice Pioneers it's what they do for fun in their spare time. Foundational voice Pioneers have the courage to make difficult decisions, and delivering the vision will always override the personal needs of any particular individual. Achieving the vision defines the team, although invariably the team that began the project will not be the one that finishes it! Pioneers recognize when a team member's competency has plateaued and when that individual is unable to go to the next level. They will even replace themselves if they think that that's what's required in order to achieve the strategic objective that has been set. That will probably sound harsh to other voices like the Nurturer, who puts a premium on valuing people, or the Connector, who values collaboration and achieving together. However, being able to make hard choices with people and resources is often required if the original vision is to become reality. D-Day in World War II offers an excellent illustration of this idea. Mentally replay any movie scene of Higgins boats landing at Omaha Beach in Normandy with soldiers battling to take the hill. Now imagine you're part of the first wave of men to take the beach and you're badly injured, lying in the sand. The Pioneer soldier, utterly focused on the larger mission in this scenario, would probably run straight past you and barely notice. If he were a particularly passionate Pioneer, he might say, "Stay alive as long as you can. I'll be back!"

In the end, the Pioneer, without realizing it, is saying, "We only have one objective, which is to clear this beach. If I stop to look after you, we're probably both going to die. The only chance you have to live is if I go and try to take out the machine guns and the tanks, which are firing at us from the top of the hill." A lot of voices can't do that. Can you imagine a

Nurturer running past somebody dying and in pain? They might make it a few paces past the wounded soldier before they realize they couldn't live with themselves if they left someone behind, and they'll come back to rescue him. The Nurturer might then say, "If you're going to die in pain, at least you're going to die with somebody holding your hand."

Can you see how, in this illustration, both voices are vital? We'll talk more about this balance in upcoming chapters, but for now, the point is: Foundational voice Pioneers tend to deal with the big picture. This allows them to make much tougher decisions in the interest of the ultimate objective and organization. It is not necessarily good or bad, it just is. Pioneers will sometimes force the decision that is unpopular because it's the right thing to do and then they will manage the unpopularity of the decision because they are hardwired to be able to do so.

The Pioneer is also incredibly compelling, rational, and logical. They almost dare you to disagree with the sheer genius of the strategic logic that lies behind their plan. Therefore, when they speak, it's often quite hard to argue with or find flaws in their ideas because they have lived and breathed their solution or plan and have thought about every possible scenario. Pioneers hate losing more than any other voice. The Pioneer lives by these words spoken by a true Pioneer, Teddy Roosevelt:

> It is not the critic who counts; not the man who points out how the strong man stumbles or where the doer of deeds could have done them better. The credit belongs to the man who is actually in the arena, whose face is marred by dust and sweat and blood; who strives valiantly; who errs, who comes short again and again, because there is no effort without error and shortcoming; but who does actually strive to do the deeds; who knows great enthusiasms, the great

devotions; who spends himself in a worthy cause; who at the best knows in the end the triumph of high achievement, and who at the worst, if he fails, at least fails while daring greatly, so that his place shall never be with those cold and timid souls who neither know victory nor defeat.

Pioneers don't quit easily. When the team is getting a bit weary and saying things like, "Are we going to make it to the end? Are we going to succeed? Maybe it's time to call it a day," the Pioneer will demand, "We go again." Because in the end, giving up is not really in their DNA, and they will keep hammering away until they break through whatever barrier is standing between them and the vision.

Pioneers love to work. They love to build efficient, systematic, repeated processes because they know that groundbreaking innovations don't occur on a single day but rather through the use of consistent plans and problem solving. Work really is their primary identity, achieving the vision they set themselves. Often what that means is that they will drive hard, and they will work until the goal is met. That capacity and stamina is another hallmark of the Pioneer.

## What They're Really Asking

Pioneers are always thinking. They tend to arrive at work earlier than most and to have thought through every scenario from several angles. Here are the internal questions, then, that they tend to ask themselves:

- "Who says we can't?" Most Pioneers understand how to align resources, people, and money to accomplish something big. They really don't understand limitations, unlike some of the other voices.

- "Are you challenging my competency? Are you competent?" Offense is invariably the best form of defense for Pioneers; they are always assessing the competency of others and discerning whether they truly have what it takes to succeed.
- "Have you got a proven track record of success?" This is similar to credible competency, but a bit different in that Pioneers trust experience. If someone has done something before successfully, then there is a good chance that he will do it well again.
- "Do you really not get it?" Pioneers believe they are always clear in their communication and find it hard to comprehend why, once they have explained the plan, other members of the team might still have any questions or concerns.

Pioneers can often be slightly intolerant of the time it takes people to realize the genius of their logical, strategic plan. They might then infer their superiority with this type of thought: "We could short-circuit the next hour by you just agreeing that I'm probably right." Again, this sounds smug, but as Pioneers who've seen the error of their ways when this type of overconfidence has created unnecessary drama, it's valuable to know that these really are the thoughts running through the heads of even the most well-intentioned Pioneers.

Most Pioneers, left to their own devices, will seek to recruit highly talented and competent people who are self-starters and don't need to be spoon-fed. They try to avoid the relational drama that comes from managing insecure emotionally needy people. Pioneers dislike weakness in themselves and others as it presents a barrier to progress and achieving their goals.

**What Is the Potential Negative Impact?**

Because the voice of Pioneers is so strong, they usually have the capacity for the greatest good in terms of scale but also the greatest potential for damage if they don't manage their engagement with others. An immature Pioneer can often appear incredibly arrogant with a very me-focused agenda. Particularly early in their careers, it can feel like they're elbowing their way past other people, because in the end, they want to fulfill their potential. They want to maximize their leadership opportunity.

The immature Pioneer has a hard time hearing all the other voices clearly. Where decision-making is concerned, they tend to be objective thinkers more than consensus-building feelers. Their world revolves around their agenda and they don't naturally make much time for other's dreams. They tend only to be interested in people whose competence they respect and who are willing to engage in logical, rational argument.

Immature Pioneers tend to critique too quickly, stifling debate and creating an adversarial culture where only certain voices feel equipped to respond to their "back me or fight me" challenge. They rarely spend time on the social and relational niceties that other voices see as necessary or enjoyable. Immature Pioneers have to learn to begin meetings with pleasantries and personal exchanges like, "How are you?" or "How is your family?" which seem like a waste of time to the Pioneer. They prefer to focus on the immediate task at hand, and this can make other voices feel undervalued.

Pioneers also don't like weakness in themselves or others and can even see illness as a weakness in a teammate or employee. We are not saying that Pioneers do not have emotions, but rather because they are so strategically task oriented they will often miss the emotional or social cues of other people or situations.

Most Pioneers will throw their idea on the table first to see if anyone will disagree. The immature Pioneer often interprets silence as agreement, but what it really means is that everyone already knows that the Pioneer has made up his mind and that to confront him could be dangerous to their immediate health and long-term career.

Pioneers will also test the validity of an idea by critiquing it to see if it holds up under scrutiny. While this is a very natural seeming behavior for the Pioneer, for the other voices receiving the critique, the results can be damaging if the Pioneer isn't self-aware of the strength of her voice. We'll talk more later in the book about the tendency of Pioneers to blow up others' ideas with the verbal version of a shoulder launch grenade. Calling out the potential negative impact here is setting the stage for greater understanding later.

Pioneers love 4th Gear task mode and 5th Gear focus mode (we wrote about this in depth in our book, *5 Gears: How to Be Present and Productive When There Is Never Enough Time*). The Pioneer work ethic and task focus can be intense, as it can appear that the Pioneer is demanding this same level of work throughout the leadership team. "Why don't you want to work 80 hours? What else have you got to do?" is the common thought process of a task-obsessed Pioneer. The immature Pioneer doesn't understand that for the vast majority of people, work is part of what they do, but they're not defined by it. Immature Pioneers often exclusively define themselves by what they actually do and achieve. Their work often becomes their identity. (Note: we will explore the downside of this kind of behavior in chapters ahead.)

Pioneers tend to value other Pioneer voices or those who are at least prepared to spar with them. However, the immature Pioneer will keep other Pioneers at a distance in the same way that two bulls keep to their own pastures!

Mercifully, only 7 percent of people have Pioneer as their foundational voice, which Pioneers usually like because they think of themselves as unique, anyway. We know this to be true as both of us have Pioneer in our top two voices. Here is Todd Milby, a mature Pioneer from Columbia, South Carolina, sharing his breakthrough as he is moving to becoming a leader worth following:

> The 5 Voices went beyond a mere personality profile; it showed me how nature, nurture, and choices have all woven the fabric of how I behave as a leader. I began to learn how to communicate with other voices in a way that I could influence and lead with greater impact. For the first time I began to see what it was like to be on the other side of me. At first, I must admit it wasn't pretty. In fact, it was very humbling. I needed to try to communicate in their voices in order to connect with them. The result was often significant relational breakthrough and a mutual feeling of being heard and understood, which led to greater influence and impact.
>
> The transformation then spread to my 10-year-old son. For the first time, I was learning to connect in ways I had never been able to before. Although I had obviously always loved my son, I began to see a transformation in our relationship because I began to value his Nurturer Creative voice. He then felt more valued and loved, which liberated our relationship. By understanding the dangers of my Pioneer voice and valuing others, I am seeing breakthroughs that I have always longed to see.

## Discovering the Pioneer Voice

We have just taken you through what sounds like a lot of negative Pioneer attributes, but don't worry. Pioneers have deep reserves of self-confidence and actually enjoy any challenge that will help them improve their performance! Remember, though, that the Pioneer is the gifted voice of future vision and strategic thinking, and teams without a Pioneer voice rarely achieve their full potential. The key is for Pioneers to be healthy. Here is a story of Nick's personal discovery:

> The quote on my online profile is (I now realize) classic Pioneer: "Everything is possible!" The 5 Voices tool was spot on for me—succinct, clear, and really easy to identify my natural voices. The big aha for me was learning that one voice is not better than another and how important it is for Pioneers to put time and effort into learning what it's like to be on the other side of them. I am learning about the impact my natural tendencies can have and how I can access those voices that are much harder for me in order to be more balanced in my communication. The idea of socializing with my team and spending time with no agenda was a surprise, together with the realization that it's not necessary to drive people so hard—not everyone wants to work as hard or as long as I do, and that's okay. I didn't realize how competitive and ambitious I appeared to others, particularly my peers. I am working on speaking less, celebrating every success, having quality family time, listening more, and holding back on firing verbal assaults. There are so many areas for Pioneers to work on, and already there are many positive changes for me and the people around me.

Like this leader, certain people resonate immediately with our descriptors of the foundational Pioneer voice, while others have had their voices muted through nurture or choices. With that in mind, listen to Jane Fardon from Sheffield, England, describe how she is learning to thrive in her Pioneer voice:

I am wired to be a Pioneer but grew up in a family with a Nurturer/Guardian father. I can vividly remember being told many times, "Jane, you have to learn to follow through. You must finish what you started. You can't keep starting new things without finishing what you've already begun."

Some of this was due to childish tendencies of not wanting to keep going when it got tough or boring. But what I didn't realize at the time was that my gifts and wiring meant I was much better at setting something up or taking something already established and building it out to the next level, than I was at maintaining the status quo or running the day-to-day. Many years later the conflict between my foundational voice and the voice of my nurture played out very vividly.

I had set up a cosmetics business, and the market was very tough. After five years of hard work I knew in my heart that it wasn't going to work and we should probably just cut our losses. While this is the nature of business at times, every voice of my nurture shouted loud in my head. "You must finish what you started. You can't walk away on a job half done." The killer phrase was, "You never stick at anything!"

My natural, foundational Pioneer voice was telling me to make the tough decision, but it was in direct conflict with the voice of my upbringing.

After two years I finally gave myself permission to make the right decision: to cut our losses and close the business. In hindsight I should have hired a Nurturer/Guardian to run the day-to-day and given myself permission to make the tough decisions much sooner than I did. Now, with my past experience and my new understanding I feel confident to function fully in my Pioneer voice, and I feel secure enough to know that I also need the other voices with me if we're all going to realize a dream.

*Some of you Pioneers will use this resource to help you lower your voice and learn to understand others, while some of you will learn how to roar.*

That is exactly it. Some of you Pioneers will use this resource to help you lower your voice and learn to understand others, while some of you will learn how to roar. It is vital for you to understand what it sounds like to be on the other side of you.

If you want to mature in your Pioneer voice, then choose at least two of these insights to help you lead yourself and others more effectively:

1. Beware the intellectual superiority complex. You don't have all the best ideas; sometimes you are actually wrong.
2. Take time to truly hear the views and opinions of others on the team. There are good ideas waiting for you.
3. Please make sure your safety latch is always in place when sharing your voice. In a moment of frustration you can do a lot of damage.
4. Only 7 percent of people view the world through your eyes. Remember that winning is not the driving motivation for most people.
5. Your team members know that you are competent, but they are not convinced that you know anything about them or their life outside of work.
6. Find a Nurturer and ask him to mentor you in how he sees the world.

7. Take time to encourage someone who doesn't deserve it. This will force you to learn how to support, not just challenge, people in your organization.
8. If you are wrong, fight your initial instinct to justify your decision and deflect blame. You will earn respect and influence if you own up to your mistakes.

# How to Interact with Each Voice

# 9 ◼

# Understanding Your Weapons System

Do you remember the words of the old nursery rhyme, "Sticks and stones may break my bones, but words will never hurt me"? Wouldn't that be nice, words that didn't hurt us? The truth is that most of us have replayed in our minds the ill-spoken words uttered by others who were either careless or clueless in their speech. Humans are wounded by words like, "you'll never be good enough," or "who do you think you are?" These examples are most often spoken by immature voices that don't have a filter or an understanding that their voice carries a weapons system. And if you don't know how to handle your weapons effectively, they will cause all kinds of collateral damage.

It might sound strange to think of our voices as weapons, but we all come into the world equipped with a weapons system that is connected to our foundational voice. Each voice handles its weapons differently and some are more deadly than others! The weapons usually come through our words, both offensively and defensively. The words, used as weapons through our voice, can come through tone, volume, or tact (or lack of it). That is why we call them weapons, because they can help or harm depending on the situation.

All the weapons are deployed every day in any environment where human beings interact. Usually, teams simply accept friendly fire and allow the Nurturers to care for the wounded without analyzing what's really happening. But where the use of weapons remains unchallenged, teams function at far below their true potential. Where team members understand the impact of their weapons system and become intentional in how they deploy it, team culture and productivity will change immediately for the better.

Let's start by looking at Pioneers and their weapons system.

## The Pioneer Weapons System

The weapons system for Pioneers involves the verbal equivalent of shoulder-launched missiles (see Figure 9.1) and full-body Kevlar armor. Think Robo-Cop, except it's your spouse at a family gathering or your business partner in a marketing meeting ready to test the validity of some poor soul's opinion by blowing it up with a verbal critique, just for sport. Or it's you.

Remember the Pioneer is usually the loudest voice, and because Pioneers are always thinking, they tend to critique very quickly and with complete confidence. The Pioneer's weapons are always at the ready, as every conversation can lead to a competitive confrontation. It is almost like they are

**Figure 9.1 Pioneer: Grenade Launcher**

spoiling for a fight with most people they meet. The more immature the Pioneer, the more often this is true. Whenever they fire their verbal missiles, whether in the form of a gruff comment or a direct threat, there will always be fallout on the other side of the table. No other voice has a defense against the Pioneer's grenade launcher; once you hear the "Foomp!" the confrontation is effectively over.

Everyone else anticipates what is about to take place and begins to move their chairs away from the danger zone. Because the immature Pioneer tends to use his weapons system without filters, the team or family members keep their heads down and learn how to survive. Those that are self-preservers may whisper, "What did he expect, challenging Joe like that?"

Immature Pioneers will sit at the head of the table, weapons system fully armed, simply waiting for someone to offer an opinion they disagree with. Here are a few examples of phrases the immature Pioneer has been known to use:

> "Can someone else try to give me a solution that will actually work?"

"If you don't have anything intelligent to say, please don't
    bother."
"Do you really think that I am that stupid?"
"If you can't deliver what we need I'll find someone
    who can."
"Seriously, I should fire all of you and just start over."

The immature Pioneer parent might go so far as to say
something like, "stupid is as stupid does," or "can't you do
anything right?" These are words that can cause wounds that
will affect kids for the rest of their lives.

While other Pioneers tend to enjoy the intellectual com-
bat and happily fire their own salvos back, the rest of the voices
are simply taken out. One Pioneer executive we have coun-
seled admitted, "I thought they knew I was just giving them a
hard time. It took me a while to realize that my direct reports
didn't think my jabs were funny."

Many of you will have been on the receiving end of the
Pioneers weapons system, while others will have seen teammates
taken down in a painfully public way. After a confrontation, the
immature Pioneer will simply reset his grenade launcher and
move on as if nothing had happened. However, over time, a
culture of fear develops around such Pioneers, and their families,
colleagues, and teams tend to manage them by holding back on
giving their honest opinions. There are some Pioneers who
consciously use their weapons system to intimidate and control
people. However, in our experience, the vast majority are simply
unconsciously incompetent and are shocked to discover how
others see them. If you are a Pioneer, take the time to find out
what it's really like to be on the other side of you in a team
environment and why people fear your weapons system.

Inside their teams, it is essential that Pioneers learn to lead
with their safety catch on at all times. Their weapons should be

a deterrent rather than an imminent threat! When people see mature, self-aware Pioneers, they love to be part of their teams. Such Pioneers align people and resources, clarify objectives, ensure projects are managed efficiently, and run team meetings that are highly focused and productive. Above all else, Pioneers know how to win, and everyone loves to be on the winning team!

The Pioneer's weapons system becomes an asset when it can be deployed externally on behalf of the team. It can be used to take on external competitors and other strategic challenges that are hindering the team's progress. In this external context, it is entirely appropriate for Pioneers to use their weapons system. Pioneers are great negotiators and get the very best deals for the team. In just one set of phone calls, they can drastically reduce the aged creditor list. When suppliers aren't delivering, they are able to crack heads and get projects back on track. When mature Pioneers go into battle on behalf of their teams, every member feels more confident that the battle will be won and walks just that little bit taller.

When Pioneers use their weapons well they can move mountains. Here is Bill, a builder and business owner, stepping in to troubleshoot with a contractor in a classically direct Pioneer way: "Hey Hank, Bill here. So, where are we on the equipment repair? You promised it would be ready a week ago. I really need to talk honestly about this Hank; it's put me in an incredibly difficult position; we can't do anything until we get these two machines fixed. This is our number one priority and I need to know it's yours as well. You have two more days to get this problem fixed, otherwise I'm going to have to explore other solutions. Are we good Hank? I need to know this is going to happen."

Listen to Maria Guy from Albuquerque, New Mexico, describe how she has learned to manage her Pioneer weapons system at home and at work:

> I have learned to put the safety catch on my grenade launcher, especially where the children are involved. I immediately notice if they haven't showered or cleaned up their rooms or anything else a typical teenager might slouch on. I want to forcefully point out how disrespectful or unhealthy their behavior is until I hear a voice in my head telling my mouth, "Don't say anything. Quit talking, stop it . . . oh . . . you've done it again." Sometimes I'm able to set the safety catch on my mouth before I speak, while at other times I don't get there in time. I now understand the destructive power of my weapons system and am trying hard to improve.
>
> Out in the community or at work on the other hand, I can't stand a leadership void. Because I know myself and the power of my weapons system, I try to avoid situations where I am tempted to take charge and bring order, especially when it is not my responsibility! When a leader doesn't step up or is disorganized, I find this incredibly hard. I sniff out inefficiency and incompetence and lack of structure and clear objectives that drive me crazy. In the past my frustration has led me to take aim and fire, stepping into the leadership void and suggesting how I think things should be done. I am learning that people welcome my insights when they see I am for them and that my safety catch is on.

This is an example of a Pioneer understanding the power of her voice and doing something about it. Maturity is so valuable.

## The Nurturer Weapons System

It seems funny to even talk about Nurturers carrying a weapons system, but they have them, nonetheless. Every army has a cadre of medics who are trained to fight by serving and who carry an emergency first aid kit (see Figure 9.2). The Nurturer cares deeply for people and is always looking for ways to encourage, while being at the ready to bandage wounds (usually left by Pioneers), offering counsel and diffusing potential conflicts. Because they are the champions of people they can use their weapon—their medical kit—in all types of situations including sickness, confrontations, and the nitty-gritty of everyday work environments.

Now you know why Pioneer versus Nurturer is not a fair fight! It doesn't matter how much gauze, how many bandages

**Figure 9.2   Nurturer: Medic**

or what sort of medicine a Nurturer throws (in the form of encouraging words, gifts, hours of listening, etc.), it's not going to make a dent in Kevlar armor. Because Nurturers do not want to fight or compete, they bring what they have, which is ultimately themselves. Their ultimate weapon is to stand in harm's way and willingly offer to lay down their lives for the people and values they care most about. In fear and trepidation they will take on the voices armed with lethal weapons, declaring "I have my medical kit, who needs my help?" Such a sacrificial gesture might cause a mature Pioneer to step back and reflect again. However, the immature Pioneer is just as likely to fire his weapon and see the relational carnage as acceptable collateral damage.

While immature Nurturers can overprotect those they love and keep them from opportunities to grow through adversity, the mature Nurturer creates a loving and supportive environment where colleagues, employees, and children are empowered to seek adventure and take risks. They do so in the confidence that there will always be a safe place to retreat where scrapes will be lovingly bandaged and someone will listen to their worries and frustrations. One of our chief goals in creating the 5 Voices was for families, teams, and organizations to truly learn to value and treasure the Nurturer voice. Our society needs them more than ever.

Here's how a Nurturer from Atlanta describes the power of her weapons system:

The culture of the company where I work has always been super competitive, even though I am not personally wired that way. I serve in an HR capacity and naturally reach out to help people, new or old, to assimilate and feel a part of our organization even beyond what's expected in my job. I think it's just in my DNA. I remember my grandmother (a definite Nurturer) telling me as a child to "kill people with kindness" when they were being mean-spirited. If the bully sees he gets no reaction, he'll either not know what to say or simply move on. I've realized that as a Nurturer, I have the capacity to counteract some of the aggressive behavior of some of our staff by applying that same principle. For example, I watched one person chew out one of his teammates recently regarding an error in a report. It was unnecessarily personal. I knew the angry guy was also trying to rebound from a quarter when his quotas were really low (we work together often), and so afterward I gave the other person some support and helped him not feel like an idiot, and then I took the angry guy a latte and offered to be a sounding board. Believe it or not, he actually yelled at me too (scary!) saying something ridiculous like, "Butt out!" But I noticed him at the other guy's desk the next day offering him a doughnut. What I did didn't solve the problem permanently, but at least it got the revolving door of tension going in the opposite direction.

## The Creative Weapons System: The Creative Feeler

The Creative voice is slightly different when it comes to weapons systems. We have actually broken it up into two categories: The Creative Feeler and the Creative Thinker, as they have a tendency to act a bit differently. Those of you foundational voice Creatives who are very relational, values-focused, and people-oriented are more likely to be a Creative Feeler. Conversely, Creative Thinkers are very rational, logical, and analytical in their assumptions and decision-making.

Creative Feelers don't really believe in weapons because they feel that they are morally wrong and unnecessary. Because they are purists and spend their time working on grand visions and ideas that serve people, they tend not to understand why everyone can't just get along and resolve conflicts peacefully.

The noble idealism of Creative Feelers works wonderfully until someone violates one of their core values or attacks something or someone who is very important to them. When this happens their blood begins to boil and seemingly out of nowhere there emerges this Hulk-like monster (see Figure 9.3) ready to destroy anything and everything in its path. Once the green monster has picked up speed, it is almost impossible to stop and has the capacity to take out even the most heavily protected voices. The Creative Feeler would rather die than back down on a matter of honor or principle; it really depends on who fires first, but either way it's not a pretty sight.

Mature Creative Feelers, however, understand their tendency to lose control when provoked and work to constantly diffuse tension as they remember the damage they have done

**Figure 9.3   Creative Feeler: Hulk**
Image credit: Nestor Ferraro, January 18, 2015. Flickr.

in their immature years. Matt Keen, Head of Global Talent for Endava, describes it perfectly:

> As a foundational voice Creative I'm able to manage my frustration at not being understood much better than before. I've learned that not everyone understands what I'm trying to say—not because they're not as clever as me but because they think differently and have strengths that I don't have. Therefore, now I manage how I recharge and it's given me permission to be me while also helping me to identify and work on my weaker areas. I always recognized that plans and deadlines were important to other people, but I'd never truly understood why my totally relaxed approach to changing them in light of new priorities and information could be so frustrating to so many. Knowing yourself to lead yourself really works. It isn't easy, but it's the only way you can get the best from yourself and those around you.

## The Creative Weapons System: The Creative Thinker

The Creative Thinker functions like a Special Forces operative and carries a powerful sniper rifle (see Figure 9.4). You're not aware the Creative Thinker is aiming at you with his critique of your ideas, and when he shoots you down, you don't even see it coming. That is what the piercing logic of Creative Thinkers' critiques do to others. Because they are so analytical and rational, they are often thinking about every imaginable possibility of the current project. This is one of the reasons they are so valuable.

Here is how Matt Hyatt, from Atlanta, Georgia, describes himself:

> I'm programmed to seek and imagine possibilities, to think outside the box, and to come up with new and improved ways

**Figure 9.4   Creative Thinker: Sniper**

of doing things. I tend to intuitively see and focus on the gap that separates our present condition from an ideal future, but usually at a very high level. I might break the gap up into three or four steps, but I don't usually get caught up in the details. In fact, I have a tendency to underestimate or ignore outright the amount of effort required to overcome a challenge.

Because of this, Creative Thinkers will sit back in a meeting, quietly listening to all the various contributions. If they believe something is wrong or a key value is in danger of being violated they will quickly take aim and fire an armor-piercing round of logical critique that highlights the inaccuracy or error and swiftly turn the discussion in a completely different direction. The immature Creative Thinker, on the other hand, might sound like this: "What you are suggesting is simply wrong and here is the evidence to show you why you are wrong." Or, "didn't Susan admit at the exec meeting that you all knew the numbers were bad?"

These kinds of comments are typically accurate and irrefutable, but the immature Creative Thinker is often right and wrong at the same time. Their critique may be factually accurate but Creative Thinkers do not win many friends; their high velocity rifle takes out everyone except the Pioneer. Although people see Creative Thinkers as competent, their teammates consider them cold and impersonal, with little skill for building friendships. Sadly, many immature Creative Thinkers simply like it that way!

## The Guardian Weapons System

As mentioned earlier, the Guardian is the protector of systems, infrastructure, and money. As such, their weapons system is more like an interrogation chamber. Guardians are compelled to ask the hard questions. Mature Guardians almost feel it is their obligation, even though they know there might be negative consequences. The mature ones do it with sensitivity and everyone knows their intentions are honorable and for the overall good of the team or organization. Immature Guardians, too, ask hard questions because they want truth and justice but with no regard for the cost of their insistent probing.

Once the Guardian has someone strapped in, the interrogation can begin (see Figure 9.5). The prisoner is forced to answer a barrage of questions as the Guardian applies his or her forensic investigative skills to test the intellectual validity of the strategy or plan being proposed. The default assumption is that it won't work. At the end of the "interrogation" if the responses were adequate and compelling, the Guardian might actually be for the proposed idea, but has left the interrogated person emotionally zapped or wounded, feeling like they have been grilled to the nth degree.

Listen as a mature Guardian, Brandon Hutchins, CEO of Gaskins Engineering and Surveying in Marietta, Georgia,

**Figure 9.5   Guardian: Interrogator**

admits to his previous immature Guardian days: "Unfortunately, my Guardian voice has interrogated more people than I care to admit. I have shut down many conversations with sharp-edged questions and strong, critical fact-filled statements intended to keep things the way they had always been."

Another favorite mode of Guardian interrogation works like this. The Guardian begins with one simple question that turns into a series of stacked questions that would make the detectives at Scotland Yard proud. Examples include:

- "So, where are you on your budget?"
- "Did you download the forms from the intranet?"
- "You said we would have it two weeks ago; when should we expect it?" (At this point the question rate per minute increases to pile on the pressure.)
- "Have you met with your team yet? You know the entire budget is due in two weeks and we have a lot to do.

Didn't you miss your budget last year as well? What is the main issue that keeps your team from hitting deadline?"

From the Guardian perspective, this process allows them to truly discern the relative merits of the ideas and capabilities of the person they are interrogating. It's business as usual for them as they calmly look through their notes to make sure they haven't missed any question they'd planned to ask. They take quiet pleasure in highlighting the inconsistencies and flaws in the strategies of the more future-oriented voices.

Immature Guardians will use their weapons system like annoying younger siblings knowing that they are getting under someone's skin. Like the infamous hall monitors in junior high school, they think it is perfectly acceptable to question others in a negative and tactless way, as they are more interested in proving themselves right than in anyone else's feelings.

And so, unfortunately, Guardians are often scoffed at for their seemingly pessimistic style of communication. Mature, self-aware Guardians, however, will ask fewer questions to gain the clarity they need to move forward, aware that they have a limited window of time before people start to resent the length of the interrogation. When Guardians use their weapons systems effectively they are able to ascertain the key information and then communicate precisely and effectively for the great benefit of the team. Notice how this Guardian, Dave Loeffel from Atlanta, Georgia, has learned to hone his voice:

In addition to being mindful of my body language and tone when communicating an idea, I have made a concerted effort to be far more relational on a routine basis. I have made a point to establish a solid relationship as much as possible. Now, when I need to be direct at times, it doesn't come across as cold as before, when those relationships were not already strong. I am really beginning to understand what it sounds like to be on the other side of me.

## The Connector Weapons System

The Connector, remember, has a loud voice. Connectors thrive on activity and connections and ensuring that the messages sent externally and internally are accurate and understood by all. Their weapons system is very different from the others, one which they feel is more advanced—it is their actual connections. The Connector believes that in the new cyber world the person whose message dominates the news cycle and social media will ultimately win all battles. That is why under pressure, the Connector will use cyber warfare as his or her main weapons system.

They can push ideas out positively to thousands of people, especially when they believe in something, but the second they are crossed they can turn their social advantage to a passive aggressive version of cyber warfare. The way the Connector tends to do this is to start planting seeds of distrust or slander in the minds of other people, whether online or face-to-face. Most connectors are not doing this maliciously, but rather covertly. It usually takes some sort of rejection to cause the cyber warfare to take place.

Again, mature Connectors are using their connections for the benefit of the whole to ensure the message gets communicated or that people get drawn in to whatever the Connector is excited about. Immature Connectors actually try to prove their worth to the rest of the team by using their relational databases as their strength (see Figure 9.6). This can

**Figure 9.6   Connector: Cyber Warfare**

come out as name-dropping and might sound like this as they use their higher-level weaponry:

> "Oh yeah? Well, I was talking with Don Smith [a high-ranking figure in the organization] and he told me that we . . ."
>
> "When I was sitting in the White House last year, I thought about that very idea." Or "I would be glad to promote that to my 25,000 followers. I can make things happen, you know."

Because this can be overused by immature Connectors, they can come across as know-it-alls or braggarts, which can be very annoying to everyone on the team. Connectors do this to try to gain control, impress, manipulate, and prove the validity of the message they are communicating.

All of this is a form of bravado, which is really masked insecurity for the immature Connector.

Immature Connectors need credit and public affirmation for the way their connections and messaging skills are making things happen. Mature Connectors will use their influence and relationships behind the scenes to keep everyone aligned and on message. They know on a case-by-case basis whether they can draw from a relational bank account or if they need to make a deposit.

Connectors are extremely valuable on any team and have a powerful weapons system designed for the twenty-first century. However, their effectiveness is ultimately determined by whether they have the ability to win the trust of Nurturers and Guardians who are suspicious of their endless positivity and voracious need to sell their vision of the future. When the future-oriented voices (Pioneers and Creatives) take the time to build consensus and allow the more conservative voices to ask their questions and do their due diligence, then all things become possible. Once the whole team is aligned, the Connector is able to nuance and shape the internal and external messaging so that the whole team moves forward together, harnessing the power of all the weapons systems. Without Connectors it's easy for a team to become disconnected, as can be seen in the following story.

One of the companies with which GiANT works had no foundational voice Connectors in its executive or mid-level management. The 5 Voices allowed them to see that, historically, the Pioneers and Creatives had put their foot on the gas in their desire to move the organization forward at 100 miles per hour, while the Guardians and Nurturers had their two feet firmly on the brake, wanting to make sure that the systems and the people were safe before moving forward to what they described as an "unknown future."

Our GiANT team has worked with them to lift up the Connector voice—those who can translate and make sure the internal and external messages are clear, consistent, and engaging. It is vital for every team and organization to have a well-represented combination of voices. When you don't have Connectors, it's hard to keep the team relationally aligned and consistently on message.

Each voice has a weapons system that it brings to the table. In the next chapter we will discuss the rules of engagement and how these can change the dynamics of team meetings. When each voice is able to harness the power of its weapons system and all voices learn to truly value one another, then all things become possible. This simple sticky language will take your team to a whole new level of productivity and alignment.

# 10

# Knowing Your Rules of Engagement

By now, you have hopefully discovered your voice and begun to understand the positives and negatives that your voice brings to your team and your family. Our goal thus far has been to get you to a point of self-awareness that would cause you to look in the mirror and make appropriate adjustments. Once personal alignment to who you really are occurs, then you are ready to begin aligning the voices on your team or family.

If you can create common vocabulary and language where everyone knows his or her voice, it becomes an amazing accelerator for creating harmony and productivity. At GiANT we work with clients in both big and small organizations who know each team member's self-selected voice order. This allows the team leader to understand who they have on the team, how to set them up for success, and how to help them feel valued while communicating more precisely. Equipped with the 5 Voices language, the leader is able to ask, "How do I create the environment that allows each person on my team to bring his or her best?"

Every single voice brings a unique and essential strength to the team. If you remember back to our 5 Voices visual, each voice is equally important to the group dynamic, yet on most teams certain voices tend to dominate the airwaves and limit the opportunity to create a strong, completely aligned environment. Natalyia Higbie from Albuquerque, New Mexico, shares her insights into this very dynamic of valuing each other's voice:

> I have observed that there is no war between two Connectors if there is a Nurturer in between. I have a group I am working with, an excellent service business, which functions in a fast-changing financial environment where the majority of the leadership team are Connectors. Connectors are perfect at providing the service and presenting new changes to the customers in a way that connects with them. But when I asked them what makes their team so successful, after we had gone through the 5 Voices, they pointed to their lone Nurturer and said, "If it were not for him, we would have been in ruins long ago."

There is no such thing as accidental synergy on a team of people. Experience has shown us that most of the teams we work with function at about 50 percent of their true potential because they don't know how to harness the power and contribution of all 5 Voices. Most Nurturers, for instance, are rarely fully understood or valued in the way they should be unless someone creates the right culture. For that reason, we have developed the "rules of engagement," simple principles that every team or family unit can understand and implement immediately. We encourage you to follow the rules of engagement for a period of time and watch what happens to productivity as you learn to communicate and connect in a new way.

*There is no such thing as accidental synergy on a team.*

Marina Ulinuic from Endava shares an example of how the rules of engagement work inside an organization:

> We have regular team meetings every morning at 9 A.M. and they used to follow a similar pattern. As a Creative, I would start to share my latest ideas, the Guardian would look puzzled and start to ask critical questions to which I would become defensive. The Nurturer would try and mediate but rarely volunteer her own opinion. The Pioneer would explain why he thought we were all wrong and outline a clear strategic road map for moving forward. We all liked each other so we found a way to make it work but we never felt truly aligned. That is when we began using the rules of engagement. I would share an agenda in advance with a bullet point summary of what I wanted us to discuss, the Nurturer would get to offer her thoughts first, followed by the Guardian, and then finally the Pioneer. We committed to truly listening to each other's contributions and using the rules of engagement to keep us on track. The change was amazing and almost instantaneous; we now had the codebook that allowed us to truly hear each other.

Not everyone values the rules of engagement, especially the task-focused, hard-driving type of leader. This kind of person believes that the best way to make things happen is to get in a room and just tell people what to do. We will address why that doesn't work long term in the following chapters.

But as you'll see in Matt Keen's story of working with a senior leadership team in London, there is exponential opportunity for improved communication when there's a shared vocabulary and best practice for communicating:

> I have to admit that I had my doubts about the rules of engagement—they seemed a little clunky or too unnatural to adopt at first, but then came a very heated debate about a new service offer we were planning to develop. The people in the room were all senior leaders and were all experienced but were all failing to listen to one another. I stepped in to facilitate the session and imposed the rules of engagement as a way of trying to allow the main speaker to get his points across and to gather all the ideas and views first. People actually started to listen properly to one another rather than talking over one another. I had to step in a few times to remind the Connectors and the Pioneers to wait their turn, but by the time we finally got to them the Connectors had tweaked the suggestions into ways they could be messaged and the Pioneers had actually shifted their initial thinking and were able to work out how best to apply the ideas and approach the challenges that had been identified. Since then I've been using it more and more and finding it more and more natural. It feels weird at first like any new habit, but it really pays dividends in the long run.

With that, here are the rules of engagement. We want to help you create a team environment where all 5 Voices are heard, valued, and celebrated, and to accomplish that we are outlining two best practice statements for each voice in a prescribed order. If you follow this strategy, you will open up the opportunity to have much more effective meetings and conversations, all the while getting more buy-in and better ideas flowing. In the beginning the process can feel quite unnatural. In fact, as Matt attested, it can feel mechanical and possibly too structured. But, in the end, everyone gets a chance to play and bring his or her best contribution to the team. After a while, the process will become second nature.

The order in which everyone speaks in a meeting is deliberate. The Nurturers go first, followed by the Creatives, the Guardians, the Connectors, and then the Pioneers. Again, this can be a challenge as most teams have been functioning in a particular way for years. However, by following the rules of engagement you will open the door for the quieter voices to bring their wisdom and insights to the table and dramatically increase the level of buy-in when the final decision is made.

Yes, we are actually suggesting that you start your meetings in this order. Try it. Start with the Nurturer and watch what happens.

**Nurturer**

Here's what Nurturers need to hear from team members in order to bring their best:

1. We want to hear your opinions. Please speak them boldly.
2. No one is going to critique your ideas immediately.

If you lead Nurturers, remember that they won't want to go first. They are much more comfortable staying behind the scenes. However, if you have a Nurturer on your team and share your confidence in her voice, she will eventually get comfortable going first and be glad of the opportunity. In the beginning, Nurturers have to be reminded again and again, "We really do want to hear your opinion. You represent 43 percent of people. You bring an insight in relation to people and values that no one else will." Remind them how much you value their contribution, how much you want to hear it, and how committed you are to making sure that no one is going to critique their opinion immediately. The fear of being instantly critiqued by some of the more deadly weapons systems naturally causes quieter voices like the Nurturer to hold back or to tell you that your idea is a good one, even if they don't agree with it. If they only experience immediate critique they will shut down completely over time. Once all opinions have been shared, circling back to discuss the Nurturer's idea is entirely appropriate.

Every Nurturer needs to know that the people on their team truly value what they bring and recognize that they have no way of protecting themselves from sniper rounds, grenades, or extended interrogations.

If the Nurturer doesn't bring his wisdom and insights to the discussion, the team misses out on the perspective of nearly half the population. This is why so many decisions made at the executive level go horribly wrong when implemented. Many of the executive teams that GiANT works with have no Nurturers on them, and no one ever took the time to intentionally ask: "What does the Nurturer, who is the champion of relationships, values, and relational harmony, think about this decision we are about to make?" What looks great on a spreadsheet and whiteboard doesn't always work because it fails to take into account the greatest variable of all: human beings. Nurturers intuitively know how people at every level of the organization are going to react to a new idea; their wisdom is priceless and yet so rarely heard or, even if heard, rarely truly listened to. When Nurturers have the assurance that they are valued and that their ideas will be listened to and respected, they bring a contribution that will save teams and organizations huge amounts of time and money.

Before a meeting, remind the team who the Nurturers are. Give them a chance to share what is on their mind. Pour into them so that you get the most out of them for the benefit of your people and the team. Imagine saying this to a Nurturer: "Nancy, you are amazing. You bring things to this team and organization that are so helpful. I'm grateful every day that you remind me that people are more important than winning, that you model what it means to truly care for people and for the needs of people, and you bring a wisdom and an insight that we desperately need." Incidentally, you can tell a Nurturer that same thing every day and they'll never become arrogant! Nurturers benefit from being regularly reminded that they are valued and viewed as highly competent professionals. For reasons that remain a mystery to both of us, even though everyone around the Nurturer can see that they are brilliant and know how capable they are, Nurturers usually struggle to believe that about themselves, or that others truly want to hear what they have to say.

If you are a Nurturer, wouldn't that be encouraging? To be known and valued and have a safe place to share your views and opinions honestly and openly. However, with the freedom comes a responsibility to the group or team you are serving. Nurturers, you must learn to embrace change and help lead it. You must be careful to not become passive or function as a victim of changes that you were not a part of making. Nurturers can often become overly sensitive to change because it's always going to affect someone. Rather than be a victim, step up in confidence, shape the change you want to see, help lead it. People trust your judgment and they genuinely want to hear your opinion. Use that as a springboard for influence and speak the truth in love. When people challenge your views and opinions, they're trying to help. It's not a personal attack, they are simply bringing their best as well.

## Creative

Let's shift to the Creative world. Here are the two rules of engagement for the Creative:

1. Dream big. We want to hear your groundbreaking ideas and insights and we understand that they will be wrong sometimes.
2. We promise to ask clarifying questions to help you truly share what's on your mind.

We need Creatives scanning the horizon for what could be. The Creatives are game changers, the secret sauce, and the vanguards of what is to be. They are the ones who create the disruptive technologies or find the opportunity that is a step change in what we do. We need their ideas and we shouldn't want Creatives to play it safe by limiting how far out on the horizon they set their sights. They need the freedom to dream and create and ponder. And they don't need to be constrained by pressure from the rest of us to get it right every time. Creatives bring gold, but just like mining that precious metal from the earth, the right answer is usually buried deep and requires a refining process. The other voices play a critical role in the process of helping the Creative bring the treasure to the surface.

So how does this process work? First, Creatives need permission to get it wrong sometimes. Not everything they bring is going to be gold; there will be iron pyrites mixed in and the team has to be good with that. It's a great vote of confidence when a Creative hears, "You have permission to think outside the box. We don't mind if you're wrong sometimes, because every now and again you're going to come up with something that changes our whole world, and for that we'll always be grateful."

Creatives can often see the future but struggle with perspective so that what they see as something for now may actually be for three years' time. Other voices on the team can help them refine their ideas and constantly talk them back to reality without snuffing out their innovative fire. Creatives often struggle with communication because they spend so much time inside their heads thinking and dreaming about the future. They assume what is so real for them has been heard and understood by those around them, which is often not the case.

Clarifying questions are the key to solving this dilemma. It is imperative for the other voices in the group to learn how to ask questions that help Creatives flesh out and refine their ideas. Most Creatives rarely say what they mean the first time, and the more pressure they come under, the harder it gets for them to communicate effectively. In a really tough environment where they are going to get only one chance to share, a Creative can cave under the pressure. What comes out is usually not understood and can sound a bit like rambling abstract ideas with no pertinent or practical next steps.

It's essential for the other voices to realize that Creatives wouldn't be speaking if they didn't have something important to say. Can you imagine how frustrating it is for Creatives when no one seems to understand what it is they are trying to share? By asking clarifying questions and demonstrating a commitment to stay with the process to the end, the other voices can help to uncover the buried, potentially garbled treasure. Here are some examples:

"What I am hearing you say is . . . ." Is that what you are saying?"
"Can you tell us again what you mean by this?"
"So are you saying that you would do X or Y now?"

These types of clarifying questions really allow Creatives to bring their best.

By the third or fourth question, the Creative will invariably produce something that is of great value. Voices that challenge, "Well why didn't you say that the first time?" don't help. The Creative will then mumble, "I thought I did," and make a mental note to keep his thoughts to himself. Clearly, this is counterproductive. If Creatives know that the team is going to help them get their ideas out, they will begin to relax and the ideas will become clearer sooner.

The rules of engagement for the Creative are so freeing. They allow Creatives to bring their best to the team. You will find that teams who learn to do this well become much more effective, very quickly. All Creatives need the rest of the team to help them bring their best to the table.

Remember that in the weapon systems, we distinguished between the Creative Feeler and the Creative Thinker. The rules of engagement above apply to both types of voices. However, there are a few nuances to bringing further clarity. As the Creative Thinker communicates using greater logical clarity, the barriers to being truly heard are higher. Most Creative Thinkers will also at times cause deep offense while they are explaining their thoughts because they tend to be very cold and critical of past mistakes, and they fail to understand that others in the room will interpret their critique as personal and will, in turn, react according to their own weapons system. This combined with the fact that the first bullet the Creative Thinkers fire from their sniper rifle is invariably not what they ultimately intended to say. It's hugely important that Creative Thinkers rehearse what they are going say ahead of time and ideally get feedback before going live. The same applies to Creative Feelers; once they understand their tendency to confuse people with their communication they can develop bullet points to create a structure for their communication. Once a Creative goes off on a tangent and starts improvising it rarely goes well!

**Guardian**

Moving to the Guardian voice, here are their rules of engagement:

1. Keep asking the difficult questions. We really need to hear them even if we don't appear to value them in the moment.
2. We promise to stay engaged with your questioning for as long as we possibly can.

The Guardian goes third in the meeting flow. Guardians need to be able to direct their challenging questions to people in the room. Their role is far from glamorous, often unappreciated, but utterly essential for the well-being of the team. Remember the wisdom of the Guardian: Sometimes Guardians instinctively know if a new strategy is going to be a waste of time and resources; at other times they probe and explore until they are convinced that the proposed plan is sound. If, as leaders, we are going to steward well the people, time, and resources we've been given, then we need to allow the Guardians to do their job.

If you are a Guardian, please ask as many questions as you need and we will try to honor the fact that you are doing it on our behalf, even if it feels painful at times. We promise to watch our body language in the process so that we don't rush you or look perturbed. In return, we simply ask you to watch your tone and tact as you ask your questions. You have a gift for strategic insight but it's not always easy to receive.

Guardians invariably arrive at meetings with highlighted agendas and preparatory notes. By the time Nurturers and Creatives have shared, the notes will be even more extensive; Guardians love to have all the information at their fingertips so they can refer back to it as required. It is actually a great strength even though at times it might seem like a nuisance. When the Guardians begin their work it will actually feel like an interrogation. Brandon Hutchins has been a long time client, friend, adviser, and business partner. As a Guardian, listen to how he advised Steve and me by using his voice well: "When Jeremie and Steve were first starting GiANT Worldwide they came to me for advice. Jeremie gave me permission to ask difficult questions and shoot holes through the new ideas. It turns out, I was able to steer them back to some foundational values they had already established and help them become far more concrete in their product offerings. This could only happen because they knew I was for them and because they had learned to value my Guardian voice."

That is what a mature Guardian sounds like. Imagine if that became the norm for your team!

Nurturers, Connectors, and Creative Feelers, please actively encourage Guardians to do their work. We strongly recommend you put on your Kevlar body armor and remember that Guardians will ultimately prevent the team from wasting resources that could be used for future opportunities for the people you are so committed to representing. Nothing frustrates Guardians more than having to deal with the fallout from poor decision making in the past. Pioneers and Creatives, let the Guardians ask the questions surrounding today. They are not resistant to change and actually enjoy being part of the visioning process; they just want to make sure the decision-making process is robust and thorough. In some ways it's hard being a Guardian because the other voices can seem more exciting. Over time, Guardians can even wear themselves out with their own questions. They tend to wish that some other voice would step in and ask the hard questions so they weren't always seen as the wet blanket.

If you are game to try to build an effective team and begin valuing the other voices then take encouragement from Ryan Underwood, CEO of Tri Leadership Resources in Tulsa, Oklahoma, who has committed to using his own voice and truly valuing the others on his team:

> I'm trying to develop my appreciation of the Guardian voice so I can value them more than I have done in the past. We are now calling out, expecting, and celebrating the difficult questions from our beloved Guardians. I try as often as I can now to highlight their role, particularly for the Creative and Pioneer voices, encouraging them to "bring the challenge . . . kick the tires . . . tell us what we're not seeing." We now look forward to the iron-sharpening-iron process of the Guardians and their cousins the Nurturers. If we can get buy-in from both of them then we know the idea has the very best chance of surviving and thriving— which is the ultimate goal for everyone. And, in turn, our Guardians are growing in their appreciation of the other voices; they are learning that their critique needs to be tempered so that other voices respond more positively to what might otherwise feel like a hammer blow crushing their latest idea.

In the end, Guardians, you bring the heat with maturity and patience. We need you to do what you do, even if at times it feels a bit heavy or can seem to slow us down. We understand that you simply want the truth and are not intending to be rude as you pursue it.

## Connector

Connectors might think they can wing it, believing they can rely on their charisma and connections, but they need rules of engagement, too. Here's what they need to remember:

1. When we critique your ideas, please remember it's not personal.
2. Please promote your ideas as passionately as you can.

Don't be afraid to sell your ideas. Connectors, sell your ideas for all you're worth! Don't try and be safe. If you believe in something and you think people really need something, then be authentic and show your passion. The reason is this: If you don't believe in it we will be able to tell. If you do, then don't hide your enthusiasm or be a Guardian to your ideas. While it may drive some people crazy, most people will give you grace and enjoy your infectious enthusiasm. Make us cry. Tell as many stories as you can. Try and win us over with what you believe is important, because we know that you understand what connects with peoples' aspirations better than anybody else. When a strategic plan has been agreed upon, the rest of us count on you to shape the internal and external communication. No one can make the case more persuasively or with more energy and enthusiasm than you, so if you don't bring your best, the team or the group will be less than it could be.

Connectors spend most of their time in meetings thinking about who they know, what would be a better way to present than the way the current speaker is presenting, and how the ideas being shared are going to affect clients and people externally. A typical day for Connectors is spent looking at their contacts and calling people to connect them to a person or an idea that might help the other person. At night, they are perusing social media, making funny comments or promoting something they are excited about. Here's Steve on Jeremie, a natural Connector:

> To watch a true Connector at work is amazing. When we first set up GiANT Worldwide, almost all of our initial clients came out of Jeremie's kindergarten class and year-book contacts! He remembers everyone's names and just stays in touch. Anyone he'd ever met was happy to hear what he was passionate about—old college friends, airplane buddies, random people in coffee shops—no one is immune to the Connector's charm. He never sets out to sell anything but just naturally communicates in a way that instantly connects with the needs of the people he speaks to. Every time he goes on a journey, he returns with a new client (he just calls them a new friend). People just seem to instinctively know Connectors like them and want the best for them.

However, at times, the immature Connector can feel too much like a salesperson. "What have you got to sell this time?" others ask. Everyone remembers the past jobs the Connector has had and moved on from, the products they were selling, or the projects they were passionate about but are no longer involved with, and the people they were once enthused about that are no longer on their radar. Because of this, immature Connectors often work extra hard to prove themselves with the next deal, while the mature Connector recognizes those projects that failed and reminds others of those that were successful.

What you find is that Connectors want to be seen as true professionals, so they often try and filter their contribution through their Guardian voice, but it ends up backfiring. They try to anticipate what critiques and challenges are going to come, and it can cause their contributions to come out in much more serious, somber ways. It is much better for Connectors to simply remember that they are hardwired to understand what people need and want. Rather than being protective of their ideas, Connectors should strive to be authentic and draw on their strong emotional intelligence. If they do, they will be able to be as laser-focused in their ability to connect people to new opportunities and resources as Guardians are to protect the foundations of an organization.

So, Connectors, be authentically you, but also recognize that we will, at some point, critique what you say, and if we don't choose to accept your idea, please know it's not meant to be a personal affront. We will give you the freedom to connect; it is what you do best. But also know we're not automatically going to agree with everything you say! It might be a timing issue that causes us to wait on a project, but that is not a personal slight against you. Practice being less defensive when people say no. Don't turn toward passive aggressive behavior, but learn to be patient.

If you are a Connector, try to listen before speaking in a meeting. Take the time to hear what the other voices are saying before you jump to making connections or networking other people in.

If you are leading Connectors, release them to be themselves and watch your world expand. When they are mature and confident they can bring so many positives to a family, team, or organization.

## Pioneer

Pioneers are used to hearing the sound of their own voice, and being asked to contribute last comes as a shock initially.

However, when this loudest voice buys into the rules of engagement and adopts a humble and responsive posture the outcome is powerful:

1. Please listen to everyone else's views first before offering your opinion or critiquing the opinion of others. You go last!
2. Please be aware of the strength of your critique when you speak to others. Speak with more empathy.

Pioneers rarely like to go last. They'll only realize how rarely they've gone last in any group discussion when you actually apply this principle for the first time. They'll sit there thinking, "Surely it's time for me to speak." Pioneers might even be tempted to go first, as usual, and see if anybody else has got anything else to share. They must resist the urge. and listen to everyone else's views first.

Pioneers, no one objects to you making the final decision in the end. They actually quite enjoy the fact that you like to take the responsibility, make the hard decisions, and lead. However, if the other voices have had a chance to share openly and if they feel they've truly been heard, then your influence will rise immediately and you will get more buy-in, both of which you will most readily want.

The rules of engagement are a moment of dying for most Pioneers. Pioneers tend to force their ideas on others and drive change. When they submit to listening to the other voices first, they can feel like they are wasting time and losing influence, neither of which is true. If Pioneers are able to develop their active listening skills, they will hear insights and perspectives they have never heard before: perspectives that represent the 93 percent of the population who don't have Pioneer as their foundational voice.

Here is a story from a Nurturer describing her run-in with a Pioneer in the business she once worked in:

As a Nurturer, I used to work for an especially domineering Pioneer who had no idea of the impact he had on others. He could take out a person verbally without a second thought, and then assume the next day they would have learned their lesson and be happy to get on with it, having taken his (not so well-chosen) words to heart. While he was capable of compassion on occasions, he generally used fear and the threat of harsh words as his chosen weapons, and my Nurturer voice was completely powerless in the face of his—he had no desire for relational harmony (he just didn't think it was important in relation to the business goals) and so my preferred weapons—kindness, sympathy, empathy, humor, scented candles, chocolates—were utterly ignored and useless. On leaving that company, it took me quite a while (several years actually) to recover my sense of identity, that it was okay to use kindness and empathy in situations of conflict, that there was a place for those as well as head-on challenge.

And not only do Pioneers need to go last, they must also remember to engage the safety on their shoulder-launch grenade. Picture the Pioneer with his weapon with the safety on as he looks across the table after giving the other voices a chance to communicate. After listening to a few of the Creative's thoughts and the Guardian's questions, Pioneers may be tempted to offer a hasty critique or a sarcastic comment that would get everyone back to the point but also potentially take out the person speaking. By adopting the rules of engagement and keeping their safety on, they will look back at the end of the meeting, reflect on the tremendous progress made, and be glad they hadn't contributed when they were tempted to. This is the life of the mature Pioneer using the rules of engagement well.

The rules of engagement can be a game changer for Pioneers in terms of increasing their ability to connect with people, obtain team buy-in, and create loyal fans rather than passive aggressive enemies. When all the other voices feel empowered, protected, and valued by Pioneers, they will work tirelessly to help reach the team goal. It may be counterintuitive for highly driven, competitive Pioneers, but by going last, speaking less, and keeping the safety on they increase their odds of winning. However, it requires a healthy dose of humility and a willingness to listen to others first.

Each person has a responsibility to become mature, secure, and confident in the use of his or her foundational voice so that the team can also become secure, confident, and productive. This is our desire for every team member who reads this book; learning to share in the right voice order and using the rules of engagement will help you and your team get there.

# 11

## Voice Control— Mastering Your Tendencies

Each of us has a voice that is distinctly ours. Just like the complex uniqueness of a snowflake, your voice order comes from your own hardwired nature, the people and experiences that have nurtured and shaped you, and your choices. There-fore, while you may share the same voice order with a segment of people, none of them will have your exact upbringing or have made the same choices.

We want to help you understand and master your voice. We want you to understand how your foundational voice shapes the way you hear and experience others. We want your voice to be confident and mature, truly able to add value to everyone else in your world. Listen to how Julie Trimble, finance director at Cygnet Texkimp, in Manchester, England, describes her epiphany:

> I found the 5 Voices to be a liberating process. I'm an accountant, a role that I love. But by nature I'm not a Guardian, I'm a Connector and a Creative, and when I get the opportunity to use those voices, I thrive. Before I went through the 5 Voices process I valued my contribution in the workplace by measuring my proficiency in accounting terms (technical awareness, reporting accuracy, etc.), but now I see that I bring far more than that. I am allowing myself to forgive my shortcomings and to recognize the skills that make me so much more than just a bean counter!

When leaders begin to know themselves and lead themselves through their voice order, they will become exponentially more productive; they have a mechanism to see who they are and how their strengths fit into the big picture of the group, which ultimately helps remove insecurity in them and reduce the drama in their relationships.

## Understanding Your Voice Order

We have spent a lot of time helping you understand your foundational voice. This is the voice that all of the other voices speak through. For instance, if your foundational voice is Pioneer but your second voice is Creative, you will behave much differently than if you are a Creative foundational voice with Pioneer second. The primary difference is the way you view the world, communicate with others, and work out your ideas. You can see how this plays out with our voice order. I (Jeremie) am a Connector foundational voice with Pioneer and Creative as my second and third voices in the way I behave. Steve, on the other hand, is a Pioneer foundational voice with Connector and Creative second and third. We are both future oriented. We both need to talk out loud to process information. I am intent on making sure the language and the message will connect before fully committing, while Steve uses his voice to lock in and start moving briskly toward a goal once the general direction has been set.

When Connectors are pioneering, they are connecting with their networks with enthusiasm and collaboration, getting everyone on board, and selling a passionate vision. When Pioneers are connecting, they are always strategic; they connect with far fewer people and focus on those they believe can contribute most to achieving the agreed upon objective. Whereas the Connector Creative is a charismatic communicator sharing his good news with anyone he meets, the Pioneer Connector is focused, forceful, and almost selling with a hint of strong intensity. It may sound something like, "You need this" or "Here is what you should do." There is little opportunity to disagree with Pioneer Connectors once they have decided what's in your best interest.

When people speak we hear a complex, blended mix of all 5 Voices. In our research we have found that your foundational voice, by nature, will shape, quite significantly, what others truly hear when you're speaking. All your words are heard through the filter of your foundational voice. Each voice will then be a complex combination but spoken through the Pioneer, Connector, Guardian, Creative, or Nurturer lens.

As you were taking the 5 Voices assessment, we asked you to write down the color of each voice. If it was deep green, then it is most likely your foundational voice, and the remaining voices were shades ranging from pure green to deep red.

We also asked you to rank your voices in order of strength and ease in accessing. Your first two voices by this stage of your life are probably pretty close to green. Most people have a couple of green voices, or voices very strongly tinted that way. The last two voices are where the challenges lie. The fifth voice that you've selected is usually your nemesis voice. The deepest red voice is the voice that you know that you are incompetent in speaking and the voice you struggle most to understand and value in others.

So to recap, your first voice is the foundation and will be green. The second and third voices are usually close to your foundational voice and may have shades of green and yellow, and the fifth voice is the one that you struggle most with and will have at least a hint of red. What about your fourth voice? Well, that one is a little trickier. After presenting the 5 Voices to thousands of people in multiple countries and contexts we have found that the fourth voice is often your unconscious incompetence. It's usually the one that you think you're better at than you actually are!

In psychology, the well-known "Four Stages of Competence" identified by Gordon Training International, describes the process of how we can move from unconscious incompetence through conscious incompetence, then conscious competence to finally reach unconscious competence. As we look at your voice order we can apply the four stages of competence lens.

Looking at our voice order will help illustrate what we mean by this.

### *Steve Cockram's Voice Order*

First voice (foundational): Pioneer—unconsciously competent
Second voice:              Connector—consciously competent
Third voice:               Creative—consciously competent
Fourth voice:              Guardian—unconsciously incompetent
Fifth voice (nemesis):     Nurturer—consciously incompetent

I (Steve) am a Pioneer with a strong Connector and Creative voice, which makes me adept at starting ventures and programs, building scalable infrastructure, and selling vision and opportunity to others. I always knew my Nurturer voice was weak, my conscious incompetence if you will, but it's something I've committed to work on over the years and I've made progress, even if from a very low base! What surprised me was how limited my Guardian voice turned out to be. I had always assumed I was okay at it, but when we dug a little deeper I realized it was actually far closer to unconscious incompetence, both in my capacity to use it and value it in other people. It's been a huge area of personal development as I've learned to work on the Guardian details and systems inside the GiANT world; it's now somewhere between conscious incompetence and conscious competence, but it's taken time and hard work.

### *Jeremie Kubicek's Voice Order*

First voice (foundational): Connector—unconsciously competent
Second voice:                Creative—consciously competent
Third voice:                 Pioneer—consciously competent
Fourth voice:                Nurturer—unconsciously incompetent
Fifth voice (nemesis):       Guardian—consciously incompetent

Jeremie is a natural Connector who is constantly connecting people to new ideas and opportunities. Because of his Creative second voice he invariably sees future opportunities before I do. Because the ideas are so big and he has learned how to Pioneer throughout his life he often struggles to clearly articulate his ideas in the very beginning. While my Pioneer voice sometimes reacts too quickly, I'm learning to pull back because time and again we've come back to opportunities and people that Jeremie had been hinting at months before. Most people can see his strong Pioneer voice as he is always starting new ventures; who do you know who moved to Moscow straight out of college to start new businesses? However, when he starts new things, it's invariably to help the largest number of people fulfill their potential. This is the Connector Creative Pioneer at his very best.

Most people would think his Nurturer voice would be higher than fourth because he is such a people person. However, because he is mostly interested in future ideas of how programs are going to help people, he struggles managing the details and anticipating the caregiving-related needs of others. People assume that he has more nurturing in him than he really does. People are fully aware, however, that he has a lack of Guardian detail!

What about you? This is a worthy exercise for you to consider for your voice order and competencies as a leader. List all five of your voices here in order of most competent to least competent:

First voice (foundational):   —unconsciously competent
Second voice:                 —consciously competent
Third voice:                  —consciously competent
Fourth voice:                 —unconsciously incompetent
Fifth voice (nemesis):        —consciously incompetent

## Being the Champion

Through the 5 Voices process, we want to give you confidence and peace to be your truest self and to use your voice for good within your circles of influence. We are all complex human beings and yet we were each designed with unique gifts that are meant to encourage and help others. Your team needs you to be the best you that you can be. Your family needs you to confidently and maturely speak your voice. Moreover, each person in your circle of care, whether at work or at home, needs you to help them understand and fully develop their voice.

To do this, you must first champion your voice for the team. In the same way that the airline attendant requests that you put on your emergency oxygen mask first, before helping someone else, we encourage you to first master your own voice before trying to help everyone else.

## What Each Voice Champions

Each foundational voice is responsible for something within the team. The team or family that understands this becomes more connected and productive. Remember, in a team environment, if you know what each member of your team brings with their particular strength, you can create a space where everyone can actually bring their best.

**Nurturers:** You are the champions of relationships, values, and people. Fight for the highest possible good in others. That is what you are responsible for.

**Guardians:** You are the champions of the systems, tradition, money, and resources. Be good stewards and ask the necessary questions.

**Creatives:** You are the champions of future-oriented ideas and organizational integrity. You are the social conscience of the team. Keep trying to make your ideas understandable.

**Connectors:** You are the champions of the relational networks, external messaging, and internal collaboration. Confidently promote what you truly believe in.

**Pioneers:** You are the champion of the strategic vision. You solve problems and make tough decisions. Keep helping the team win and make sure we are alive when we get there.

For any executive team to function at its full capacity, each voice needs to be honored and represented in strategic discussions. When you are missing a specific foundational voice around your board table, recognize that fact. It may be that someone has it as his second or third voice and can bring that perspective. However, in our experience the foundational voice always brings something that voices two and three don't, so we recommend you use someone outside the immediate team as a sounding board or final filter. Every business or organization needs to champion the invaluable contribution each of the 5 Voices makes. To minimize or marginalize any of the voices is to undermine team effectiveness and your own influence, both inside and outside of your organization.

## 70/30 Principle

When people are in the right roles, on the right teams, and feeling valued for the contribution they are bringing, they invariably thrive and the whole organization benefits. However, when a person is in the wrong role for far too long using their fourth and fifth voices, they start to get worn out, becoming less and less productive no matter the size of the stick or carrot.

To help others understand this, Steve created the 70/30 Principle, which we have found very applicable in this new world of task domination. Most people have heard about the

80/20 Rule or the Pareto Principle, which states that 80 percent of the effects come from 20 percent of the causes. Said another way, 80 percent of sales come from 20 percent of clients and so on.

The 70/30 Principle, which we can dub "Cockram's Law" for fun, speaks more to our personal leadership behaviors: If you are using the voices that come most naturally to you for 70 percent of the time, you'll always have the energy to do the 30 percent of activities that require you to use your fourth and fifth voices. Put another way, if you spend 70 percent of your day doing what you are good

> *70/30 Rule: If you are using the voices that come most naturally to you for 70 percent of the time, you'll always have the energy to do the 30 percent of activities that require you to use your fourth and fifth voices.*

at and enjoy, then you can easily handle the 30 percent that is not enjoyable or easy for you.

For Steve, who is a Pioneer/Connector, his 70 percent gets met in performing strategic consulting, coaching highly competent leaders, negotiating, and apprenticing others. His 30 percent Nurturer/Guardian is having to care for the practical needs of people, repetitive manual tasks, detail work done alone like writing training curricula, editing books, evaluating spreadsheets, or reading legal contracts. When he stays in his 70 percent zone, then others get the best out of the Pioneer/Connector voice. When he spends too long functioning as a Nurturer/Guardian, stress behaviors start to take over.

What is it for you? What are the 70 percent activities that come easy to you or that you enjoy, and what are the 30 percent areas that you would rather not do or deal with?

We've observed that as people get out of balance and the percent ratios shift to 60/40, 50/50, 40/60, 30/70, they get worn out, and you will start to see productivity and engagement decline. No matter how hard they try, it's hard for people to get excited or motivated when they get that out of balance. Millions of people are stuck working in 30/70 ratio roles, spending a majority of time doing things they are not naturally good at. When this occurs, work becomes something they endure instead of something that they actually enjoy doing. When you look at people in your organization or your teams and say, "They used to be really alive and engaged and now they just look really worn out, and they're a bit more cynical, and . . ." Invariably, they've simply ended up in a 30/70 or 40/60 role for an extended period of time. They've been using their fourth and fifth voices far too much.

The 70/30 Principle is merely anecdotal; we've worked with thousands of leaders all over the world and found it to be an incredibly helpful lens. It helps people to make sense of their world and to discover when they are in the wrong roles or using voices that are not naturally theirs. Remember, the 70/30 Principle is a guideline, not a rule, and it's intended to help you gauge how alive you are. With that, let's have a look at your world. If you look across your whole life, how's the balance for you right now? What percentage of your time is taken using your first and second voices and what percentage of your time are you using voices four and five? Is it 70/30, 60/40, 50/50, 40/60, or worse?

List your percentage ratio here: __%/___%

## Cultural Bias

As a global consultancy and content creation company, we have worked with leaders in all types of settings and locations. When we begin to meet with leaders and help them unpack their complex lives, we have noticed that there are certain cultural biases that might affect the foundational voice and voice order. When we first start helping others discover their natural foundational voice, we always explore their nurture and the choices they have made, which may have caused certain voices to be ranked higher than expected. Societal pressure and culture will often sway the way you live and lead. For instance, if you happen to be a Pioneer in the United States, the culture says by nurture, "Go for it, live the dream, stake your claim." Thus, Pioneers are valued to a high degree and many people aspire to live like a Pioneer when they are really not. In Germany, however, when we asked a group of people who their heroes are or who young people aspire to be, there was silence. Only when we repeated the question did someone finally volunteer the tentative answer, "the Prime Minister?" as if out of obligation. As we unpacked the issue further we discovered that their cultural heroes were either deceased or were sporting heroes who rose to prominence for a specific period of time before fading from view. Germans have a deep mistrust of strong charismatic visionaries, and when one reviews their history it's not hard to understand why the Pioneer and Creative voices are viewed with suspicion.

In the United States, people are more comfortable with the failure of an entrepreneur; it's how you learn! The culture in Switzerland, however, is very different. If your business fails and you declare bankruptcy, the stigma will stay with you and your family for a generation or more. Can you imagine what it's like to be a foundational voice Pioneer in Switzerland? Swiss Guardians, on the other hand, love the prevailing culture—everything runs on time; it's clean; everyone dresses smartly; and the culture celebrates bankers, watchmakers, engineers, and high-end chocolate. Do you see how powerful

the oughts and shoulds of your culture can be? Ask yourself the
following four questions:

1. Which voices are celebrated in my country or community? Which voices are viewed with suspicion?
2. Which voices are celebrated in my organization? Which
   voices are viewed with suspicion?
3. Which voices are celebrated on my team? Which voices
   are viewed with suspicion?
4. Which voices are celebrated in my family? Which voices
   are viewed with suspicion?

## Mastering Your Voices for the Benefit of All

When you understand how nurture and choice have shaped
your natural voice order, you have the opportunity to truly
master your voice and function with a level of confidence and
maturity that is hugely attractive. Having mastered your own
voice, you are able to help others discover theirs. When
someone hears her voice for the first time it can be an
emotional experience just like it was in Chapter 1 with Sarah
Churman. We meet many leaders who were never allowed to
be themselves growing up; they've spent years trying to live in
an identity that wasn't really them. There are often tears when
people realize it's okay to be themselves and to use the
foundational voices they were born with.

See how Matt Keen of London shares his experience in his
family. Notice how he leverages what he knows about himself
to help shape others:

I'm a Creative Connector. My wife is a Guardian Nurturer.
Who knew that I'd effectively married my nemesis (in voice
terms at least!). The insight the 5 Voices has given us on how

people interact has been a huge help in making sure we continue to understand and appreciate one another given the pressure (and fatigue) that comes from two introverts having two children and busy jobs. I find that I use the tools and the 5 Voices within my family all the time now. When a new au pair started with our family, I used the 5 Voices to help her to understand herself and the family dynamics quicker.

The appreciation that we're all different as a result of our nature, nurture, and choices means that we have a much better understanding of our tendencies and can choose to behave differently.

Transformation happens when people begin to use the insights of the 5 Voices in every sphere of their life—it's a game changer for relational dynamics and effective communication at home, at work, and in the wider world. Learning to appreciate and value the contribution of your fourth and fifth voices will take your influence to a whole new level.

Know your foundational voice, then move on to fully comprehend your voice order. Practice harnessing your weapons system and use the rules of engagement to hear and value every voice's contribution. Once you have mastered these abilities, you can begin to help others understand what it is like to be on the other side of their voices.

Communication is pivotal, and in the next section we are going to begin to show you how the voices can effectively communicate change and vision—or not. Mastering your own voice is the first step to you becoming a leader worth following.

# Building Powerful and Effective Teams

# 12 ■

# Leading Effective Change

Picture yourself in front of a group of people, whether it is your team, family, or a volunteer group at your church or community group. You are standing there about to share some really important changes that are about to take place. Or, you may be sharing a vision of the future from your perspective to get everyone on the same page as you. There are several possibilities for how this could go. Perhaps you'll see nothing but blank stares. Or you will see heads nodding, or both. Perhaps you are surprised, after you paint a glorious picture of the future, that nobody seems motivated to take action, or seem to have not even heard you at all. Why is that?

The best leaders have the ability to communicate vision clearly and effectively, while leading people through the necessary changes in a way that allows as many people as possible to feel supported in the process and does not squander resources along the way. Sound impossible? It's not, but it requires that leaders create an environment where everyone can effectively hear the vision or idea, adapt to it, and offer his or her own suggestions. We're going to show you how to do that, how to take your understanding of your voice and tendencies and learn to communicate, make changes, and cast vision.

Here's a question for you. Which voices do you think make the most effective communicators and why? You might say, "Connectors, because they tend to be storytellers." Others may say, "Pioneers, because they're not afraid to say exactly what's on their mind." Most Pioneers, by the way, undoubtedly think they're the best communicators in any room! Take a look at the tool we've developed for teaching this concept (see Figure 12.1).

Here's the reality of which voices are most effective at communicating: We overlaid the 5 Voices onto a graph

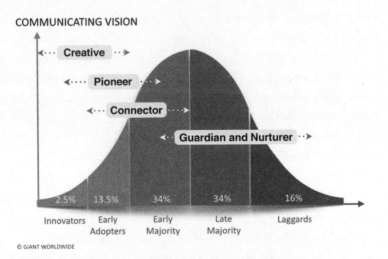

COMMUNICATING VISION

Creative

Pioneer

Connector

Guardian and Nurturer

2.5%    13.5%    34%    34%    16%

Innovators    Early Adopters    Early Majority    Late Majority    Laggards

© GiANT WORLDWIDE

**Figure 12.1   Communicating Vision**
*Source:* E. Rogers, *Diffusion of Innovations* (1962).

representing Everett Rogers' Diffusion of Innovations theory as a way to help visually illustrate why certain voices have difficulty understanding one another. Rogers' theory accounts for the way ideas and technology disperse through a given culture. When you look at the 5 Voices juxtaposed on Rogers' graph, you can see that each voice connects two groups to the right of where they started.

Notice that the Creatives are usually positioned the furthest out into the future, so they speak fluently and clearly to the innovators and the early adopters, which is only 16 percent of the population. That's the reason why most Creatives struggle to be heard when they start speaking. Only one in seven people has any idea what the Creative is talking about! And you will find that small group usually is composed of fellow Creatives who speak fluent Creative as well.

Also notice where Pioneers fall in their ability to communicate. Pioneers only reach half the innovators and half the early majority, which is 31.75 percent of the population. This is another dying moment for every Pioneer because they inherently believe that everyone around them will understand anything they say. At this point most Pioneers are thinking, "Well, I'm not an average Pioneer. Some Pioneers might have issues communicating, but not me." The reality is that Pioneers reach just over a third of people, which means that two-thirds of people, when hearing a Pioneer speak about his vision, think the Pioneer is offering them an opportunity to die in battle for that vision—to spend their lives and resources willingly so the Pioneer can achieve the ultimate objective that he's set for his latest conquest.

Connectors, interestingly, reach all of the early adopters through most of the early majority, which is roughly 47.5 percent of the population. Connectors really are the bridge between the very future-oriented people and those on the back half of the bell curve of the graph who tend to be, by nature, more present-minded and conservative. Connectors have a huge communication advantage, as they can be the bridge between the future and the present.

Guardians and Nurturers reach about half the early majority, all the late majority, and about half the laggards—an unfortunate name, which we will blame Rogers for as this outdated language is not our choice. No one wants to be called a laggard; that terminology implies laziness, but a more accurate definition is "cautious or suspicious of change" and thus the category is still relevant to the conversation.

Guardians and Nurturers make up 73 percent of the population. However, when they speak, only 59 percent of the population will hear them according to the Rogers bell curve (half the laggards are opposed to any change regardless of how it's communicated). Think about that for a moment. If you were to ask people in most organizations who are the most effective communicators, very few would name Guardians and Nurturers as those who would be able to be heard by the largest number of people, but it's true—59 percent!

Consider the following story, which is based on the experience of a friend who is an archetype Pioneer (meaning, it's the greenest of green foundational voices for him). Let's call him Bob. He's married to Liz, who is a foundational voice Nurturer who is wired completely opposite to him. Early in Bob's life, he thought he was highly competent at pretty much everything. At one point he was trying to pitch a vision to about 300 people: an opportunity to invest in an exciting new venture. Bob staged the full dog and pony show to get these people to envision the incredible opportunity he was inviting them to join in. As he was wrapping up he felt good. In his mind the presentation had been compelling, and he'd given it everything he had in terms of energy and charisma. He thought his close was really strong and he ended with the challenge, "Okay, who is in?" There was a stunned silence and three people raised their hands. As a Pioneer, Bob thought their hesitancy had nothing to do with him. So he asked again, "How many people are on board?" You could hear crickets. This Pioneer was dying on the inside and he didn't know why. He was thinking, "What is wrong with these people?" Out of nowhere, Liz walks to the side of the stage, and Bob says to himself, "Great, in my moment of utter despair and darkness I'm about to be humiliated by my wife." She asked if she could share a few words and at this point Bob didn't really feel he had anything to lose. Liz spoke very quietly, had no presentation and no fireworks:

> I know what you're all thinking. I was thinking exactly the same about three months ago when this idea was first mentioned as a possibility across the kitchen table. I confess my initial thoughts were far from positive; "yet another hair-brained scheme where we all get to lose our money." And then she said, "But you know, over the last three or four months I've listened to all the conversations, I've asked a lot of questions and fully engaged with the process. And stunned as I am to come to this conclusion, I actually think this may work and I'm prepared to invest some of my own money in this. I don't know whether that is helpful to any of you.

Bob is flabbergasted, thinking, "Really? I mean, it was a nice gesture, but it was so low-key and lacked enthusiasm. Surely no one is going to change his mind at this stage." However, it was worth a try so he asked one more time, "Well, in light of what you've now heard from Liz and me, how many of you may be interested in investing in this opportunity?" Half the room put their hands up! One person stood and said, "Liz, I've always trusted you" (*read* not your husband!). It was the archetype Guardian, the one who carried the budget around with a red pen. As this person continued, he explained, "I've always trusted your judgment. If you've done your due diligence on this and you think it will work, that's good enough for me. I'm in. I loved the vision, I just wasn't sure it was safe." Someone else stood up and said exactly the same thing, "You're an attorney and I trust your judgment. If you've asked all your questions then I'm in as well."

This was a humbling but massively significant aha for a then-immature Pioneer. When it comes to communicating vision it is not about the boldest voice or the grandest vision, but rather, it is simply about understanding your audience and which voice or voices are able to connect most effectively with the audience. You might have the best idea in the world, but if the audience walks away puzzled and perplexed, then you have just wasted months of work and lost all momentum. I am certain that every Creative, Pioneer, and Connector reading this book will have their own similar stories to share where they thought they had communicated a compelling vision of the future only to hear the same crickets that Bob heard. I am also certain that those of you with a foundational voice Guardian or Nurturer are smiling to yourself!

> *When communicating vision it is not about the boldest voice or the grandest vision, but rather, it is about understanding your audience and which voice or voices will be able to best connect with the audience.*

When you begin to know yourself, you can begin to lead yourself. Most foundational voice Pioneers assume that they are right, and, therefore, it's only a matter of time before others will relent and commit to aligning behind their vision. It's important to remember that for people on the other side of the table from a Pioneer, it can often sound like they are being sold something or ordered around. The net effect of this is people reacting defensively, turned off by what the (overly) confident Pioneer is saying.

When you put this together you begin to understand how the forcefulness and innate confidence of future-minded Pioneers can actually cause everyone else to pull back instead of pressing forward. In Bob's story, the Nurturer was able to connect with the majority of the audience, provide some different insights, and gain the trust of others who shared her same voice. Ultimately, we always hear our own foundational voice much more easily than we do the others. Whether you communicate less effectively than you realize or have an untapped ability to influence, all of the voices benefit from understanding the dynamics of how we hear one another.

## Communicating Effective Change

In addition to knowing our limitations and opportunities for communicating, we also need to develop the capacity to use our voice and deploy others to manage change effectively.

In a perfect world, Pioneers and Creatives would be out on the front lines, focused on and exploring future possibilities. Connectors would be trying to message the opportunity, getting everybody on the same page and fully aligned. Nurturers and Guardians are connected and engaged but invariably toward the back because they want to make sure it's safe and that the people, money, and resources are being taken care of. Sadly there's no such thing as a perfect world or a perfect organization. In reality there is always a stretch between the Pioneers and the Creatives who want to get

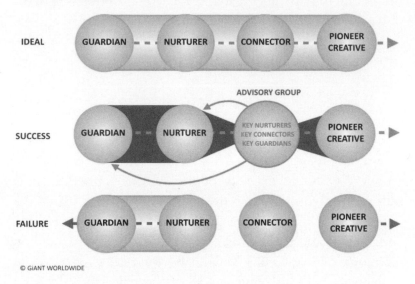

**Figure 12.2   Leading Effective Change**

to the future yesterday, and the Guardians and the Nurturers who want to make sure any change happens safely and at a pace everyone is comfortable with.

For organizations to succeed, there is a certain level of tension that has to exist between these two groups. And tension is different from friction. Think about a suspension bridge: It's the opposing forces of the cables and girders that allow the bridge to do its job. Healthy tension is a success criterion for teams and groups, too, and when all voices are heard and valued, the resulting synergy is amazing. That rarely happens, however. The Pioneers and the Creatives tend to get so frustrated at the pace of change that in a moment of impatience they put their foot flat on the gas pedal, convinced that once the Nurturers and Guardians see the future they'll be grateful. In so doing they create massive stress inside the organization. The Connectors try and hold everyone together for as long as they possibly can, but they can only do this for so long.

As Pioneers and Creatives drive hard toward the future, they fail to understand why Guardians and Nurturers have their feet firmly on the brake pedal and are pulling at the parking brake for all they're worth. The Connectors try and keep everyone engaged and talking, but once opposing camps have been firmly established, it's only a matter of time before the disconnection occurs. How many organizations have you been part of where such a separation has happened? The Guardians and Nurturers get together and talk amongst themselves saying things like, "There is no way that I am going to let them do this again. Do you remember what happened last time? They are clueless!" The Pioneers don't even talk; they just drive forward and use bullying phrases like, "I don't care what it takes. We are going to make this happen. If they can't buy in, then we will find someone to take their place. No one is irreplaceable."

Tossing words like these around in an organization is like driving a car with one foot fully throttled down on the gas and the other fully pressing on the brakes. The car will go, but it spins its tires, makes a horrific noise, and eventually will blow up.

It's essential we understand that 73 percent of people are hard wired to put their foot on the brake when change is being considered. It's not that Guardians and Nurturers object to vision and progress; they actually enjoy shaping the future. They just need a clear understanding of the details and future direction before they are willing to take their feet off the brake. This causes huge frustrations for Pioneers and Creatives, and if they don't understand and value the Guardian and Nurture contributions it will always lead to problems. Productivity declines, morale sinks, and several hours a day are spent on the drama of disconnection between the two groups.

At this point, Pioneers and Creatives have three choices, two of which are good:

1. Create an advisory group and use complementary voices to help shape internal and external communication.
2. Have a Guardian or Nurturer share the vision of change with the whole organization.
3. Press on regardless, assuming that the Guardians and Nurturers will eventually fall into line.

## Creating an Advisory Group

An advisory group for Pioneers and Creatives is exactly what it sounds like—a group of people who are able to help shape and refine communication and strategy before it goes live. Ideally, the advisory group would consist of Guardians, Nurturers, and key Connectors, or whichever voices come third, fourth, or fifth for the particular leader. For instance, the president of the United States has a press secretary, chief of staff, and other advisers who play this same role of ensuring that what the president shares will connect with the largest percentage of the population. The same goes with you and your advisory group.

If you choose to create an advisory group, then you are choosing to humble yourself and slow down. You may want the organization to move with you at 70, 80, or 100 miles an hour, but the truth is that if you disconnect the Nurturers and Guardians you are bound to fail. Most Pioneers run ahead, climb another mountain, and look back scratching their heads saying, "I thought I was so clear. Why isn't everyone with me?" Pioneers, hear us: If you slow down to reconnect with 73 percent of your people you won't be able to run 100 miles per hour, but you will be able to get to 35, which is so much faster than zero. An African proverb comes to mind here,

"If you want to go fast, go alone. If you want to go far, go together."

One executive we worked with in a senior care center realized that he was driving people crazy with his big ideas in a very conservative culture. As a Connector/Pioneer, this leader was wearing out his board and causing huge frustration within his team; in his desire for change he appeared not to be recognizing or honoring all they had already accomplished. He decided to create an advisory group with a key Guardian, two Nurturers, and a Connector. The result, while it took a few months, was that he rebuilt trust and began to slow down so that he could actually hear his team and let them hear him. They realized that he wasn't as far out as they thought. Though it feels slower, it actually speeds up the organization as everyone begins to move in the same direction.

Here is how an advisory group works well. The Pioneer or Creative (sometimes Connector) will invariably share his or her grand vision. The Nurturers and Guardians will take a sharp intake of breath and say, "Well, if you shared that it would be an utter disaster." Both Pioneers and Creatives initially assume that the more cautious voices are overreacting. However as the Nurturers, Guardians, and Connectors begin to share their insights and ask their questions, the Pioneers and Creatives become increasingly grateful. This is the process of maturity and humility. The goal is to create a new discipline where the foundational voice Pioneers, Creatives, and often the Connectors commit to never going live with a new vision until at least the Guardians and Nurturers have had a chance to help shape the communication. It takes longer. It often feels constricting because the agreed upon communication is rarely what the Pioneer, Creative, or charismatic Connector would have chosen to share.

The second alternative for effectively managing change is to have a Guardian or Nurturer share the vision instead of the more future-oriented voices. If you really want to see change, this has proved to be the most effective strategy. Let the Nurturers, Guardians, and Connectors help shape the vision with you, then empower these voices to communicate to the wider organization. The Pioneer or Creative can set the stage by painting the big picture for a few minutes before handing it over to the Guardian, Nurturer, or Connector. At this point, some of you Pioneers will likely be thinking, "This is ridiculous. That would never work." Jeremie tells a story about a time this happened when he was leading GiANT Impact in Atlanta, Georgia:

> Several years ago I was running the Leadercast and Catalyst Conferences out of our GiANT Impact division. I am a Connector/Pioneer but was using my Pioneer voice most of the time. When I would share a big vision about the future, I thought I was hitting home runs, until I talked to my COO, Chris Ediger. He would share how badly I missed connecting with the audience and I would scratch my head in disbelief. "You're stressing out all of the staff every time you come back from lunch with a million new ideas. Why don't you let me share your ideas," he would say, as I was constantly changing direction and oversharing vision. I actually agreed with Chris as I realized my disconnection was real. Thus, I began shifting time by speaking for less than 10 minutes, while Chris would share the details for 30 minutes or more. No offense to Chris, but I thought I was a much better speaker with my rah-rah style. What I realized was that in that season Chris was actually a much better communicator. Speaking wasn't as important as communicating. This caused a humbling period in me and an easier season for our employees.

When a Guardian or Nurturer stands up and communicates the change heading toward the future, everyone thinks, "If you think it will work, then I am in." People trust that the Guardian has looked at all the details and that the Nurturer knows it will work for the people. Trust is built because of the perceived due diligence that has been done, which allows other people to take their feet off the brake a bit more.

The third option, which we do not recommend, is for Pioneers or Creatives to double down, put both feet on the gas, and drive through the change, convinced everyone will eventually thank them for their vision and leadership. However, doing this simply marginalizes at least 73 percent of the organization. We know that some of you are thinking, "Jeremie and Steve, there are times when you need to do that." Granted, there are rare occasions when the Pioneer needs to turn left sharply and share the plan quickly and confidently. However, we are talking about establishing principles that Pioneers and Creatives will adhere to in 95 percent of situations. It is crucial to get buy-in from all voices if you are going to lead effective change. Remember, the present-minded voices have long memories and your reputation sits squarely in their minds. Do the right thing.

When it comes to communicating vision, effectiveness of communication, and leading change, what are the big ahas as they relate to you and your world? What changes do you need to make?

Take some time to plan your advisory group. After looking at your voice order, who do you trust to be in your advisory group? Who do you think might be the best fit for you for an advisory group based on your personal voice order? If you are a Pioneer/Connector, for instance, it would be best to find a Nurturer, Guardian, and Creative. They could be on your team already or you could be married to one of them. It could even be a friend who knows about your organization. Make a list of who those people might be for you.

Our goal is to give you practical tools to help you lead more effectively for you and your teams. The next concept reflects this desire to help you connect, motivate, and move people to another level.

## Building the Bridge

After years of working with leaders, we have created a powerful visual tool to help the future-oriented leaders connect with those who are more focused on the present. The tool we want to introduce to you is called Build the Bridge (see Figure 12.3). The idea is that when it comes to envisioning the future, Guardians and Nurturers need to see that there are clear steps on the bridge for everyone to walk across. The future-oriented voices (Pioneers, Creatives, Connectors)

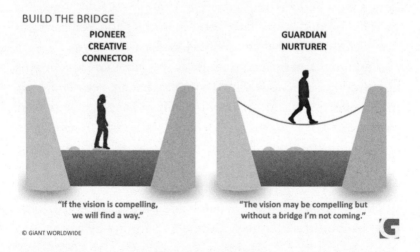

BUILD THE BRIDGE

PIONEER
CREATIVE
CONNECTOR

GUARDIAN
NURTURER

"If the vision is compelling, we will find a way."

"The vision may be compelling but without a bridge I'm not coming."

© GiANT WORLDWIDE

**Figure 12.3   Build the Bridge**

are less concerned with how they will get to the other side. Their attitude tends to be, "If the vision is compelling, we will find a way." It doesn't matter if they have to jump across rocks or step on a crocodile, they will figure it out as they go.

Most intuitive Pioneers and Creatives do not fully comprehend the practical concerns of the Guardian or Nurturer. Pioneers and Creatives ready to head to the new frontier become dumbfounded as they realize that no one is following along behind. By the way, our experience shows that Guardians and Nurturers actually love vision as much as any of the other voices do, but they do ask the question, "How do we make sure it's safe for me to bring all the people that I feel responsible for to the other side?" The vision may be compelling to them, but without the bridge they simply are not coming.

Most foundational voice Guardians and Nurturers can recall a time, when, against their better judgment, they trusted the future-oriented voice and followed without doing their usual due diligence. The tragedy that unfolded is seared forever in their memories; every Nurturer remembers the people who drowned, those who got eaten by the crocodiles, and the number who had to be treated for hypothermia having been rescued from the water. Their lifelong vow is now, "No matter how compelling the vision or how persuasive the leader, I'm never, ever leaving the safety of the cliff with my people unless I can see a bridge that will get us safely to the other side." Every Guardian remembers the fight to stay afloat and the tragic moment when all the money and resources that had taken years to accumulate sank to the bottom of the ocean because somebody didn't build a bridge. They vow never to make the same mistake again no matter how much pressure they are put under.

This language should help all the voices to understand whether they have effectively built the bridge or can at least see the bridge under construction. It's also important to note that Guardians and Nurturers don't want a bridge built for them, they actually want to be a part of building it so they know it is sturdy and sufficient.

In concrete terms, building the bridge might mean ensuring that the IT infrastructure is built before we start selling the products that require it and that all divisions in the business are fully in the communication loop. Guardians and Nurturers see what the Pioneers, Creatives, and Connectors don't tend to see—the reality of today. They know where the weak points are and can save a lot of pain if they are listened to. They simply want to see a way for the organization to move forward securely; they need to know that 100 percent of the people can safely cross the bridge into the new future.

Here are a few questions for the future-oriented voices to ponder:

1. Do you truly value the contributions that Nurturers and Guardians make?
2. Have you created opportunities for them to help shape the future all the way through the visioning process?
3. Have you got an advisory group in place that will help craft your internal and external communication?
4. Do you need to have someone else communicate your vision so that more people can understand and buy into the change program?
5. Have you invited Guardians and Nurturers to help build a bridge so that they can feel safe joining you on the journey?

Slowing down is actually speeding up. The best leaders know this. Those who have led the implementation of big visions or masses of people know intuitively how to get buy-in and how to move people effectively across wide rivers. Once they have people moving they can then slowly pick up the pace; this is the power of momentum. It is counterintuitive for Pioneers and Creatives, but the faster they want to travel the slower they have to start the process.

These three visual tools are easy to understand and hard to implement. However, they could be game changers for many of you with future-orientated voices who desire to be more effective leaders. It starts with you knowing yourself and then leading yourself. This leads to maturity when you learn to value the contribution that everyone brings. Effective leaders become intentional about creating a context where everyone is able to bring their best. Leadership is hard enough. A lot of immature leaders make mistakes and burn capital they didn't need to in their enthusiasm to reach the future too soon. Do the hard yards well and watch your influence increase; it's the best way to see your vision become reality.

# 13 | ■
## 100X Team Challenge

By now, you should be very familiar with your foundational voice, its weapons system, and your voice order. You should be aware of how the lenses of nature, nurture, and choice have all played their parts in shaping your leadership behaviors and how, through your voice, you hear and communicate vision and change. Put simply, the more you know yourself the greater your capacity to lead yourself.

Before we shift into thinking specifically about your team, take some time to reflect on these questions:

- Do you know yourself well enough to lead yourself? If not, then others will have a hard time following you.
- Do you know the individuals on your team well enough to lead them appropriately? What are their tendencies? What motivates them?

- Are you willing to take the time to apply these leadership principles precisely and relevantly with your team?
- Do you understand what it sounds like to be on the other side of your voice?
- Do you value the voices that are different from yours?

To this point our primary focus has been applying the insights of 5 Voices to what we call the Self Circle of Influence; we know that leaders define culture and as such, transformational change here will deeply impact the way we lead in our families, teams, organizations, and communities. Let's now shift the focus to the Team Circle of Influence.

## What Does Your Team Really Look Like?

So, how well do you know your team? Do all the team members know that they are valued and understood? If you were asked to describe your team culture today, how would you answer? As you think about your answers to these questions, here are some of the most common responses we encounter in our work:

- "My team is brand new as we have just gone through another re-structuring. We don't have time to meet often, we are given big goals and short deadlines. We function as individuals far more than a team."
- "Our team is a hodgepodge of industry guys who focus on protecting themselves and their jobs by constantly one-upping each other, trying to prove what they know."
- "Our CEO wants to be the center of attention. Our 'team' is basically full of 'yes' guys who walk on eggshells

and don't want to upset our founder CEO. We have realized it is easier to just go along than try to change or persuade him."

- "Our team is solid. We get each other and for the most part allow everyone to play his or her role so that we can hit our goals. I really like my team."
- "My team is one other guy and me. We are so busy knocking out tasks that we don't spend much time developing ourselves or us as a team."

Which of those sound most like you and your team? Are you positive or negative, overall?

Everyone wants to be known, respected, and appreciated for the effort they bring to the table, and the 5 Voices is a powerful lens for helping accomplish this. Most dysfunctional teams give little space for this type of recognition that is so crucial for the magic of trust. Pat Lencioni, bestselling author of *The Five Dysfunctions of a Team*, deals directly with this dysfunction in his book, using a parable of team dynamics. He specifically points out that, "The ultimate test of a great team is results." We believe that knowing your voice and the voices of those you lead is the most effective route to creating a great team and the results that come with that team.

Now, let's get to the next level by diving into the components that could make your team healthy and effective. To do that we are going to help you to get to the current reality of your team, see the gaps, and make some changes.

For each of the following criteria, give your team a score between 1 and 100, where 100 is perfection and 1 is a complete disaster. Please write the number that best defines your team's effectiveness. For instance, you could list your team as 70, 60, 85, 92, 50, and 88. Be honest and real as you evaluate your team.

- Alignment: The team is in agreement, working toward the same goal.
- Synergy: There is a combination of interaction, cooperation, and effort.
- Performance: Everyone understands what success is and is hitting goals.
- Communication: There is clarity and a clear line of communication.
- Capacity: The team is growing and is not limited by competency.
- Relationships: Overall, the team is fighting for everyone's best effort.

Now, add up the six individual numbers and divide the total by six. This will give you a snapshot of your current team health percentage. For instance, the above numbers of $70 + 60 + 85 + 92 + 50 + 88 = 445 \div 6 = 74$ percent. In this example, the team is 74 percent effective.

There is no such thing as a perfect team because teams are made up of complex, flawed individuals like all of us; however, the task of all leaders is to move their teams' effectiveness percentage as close to 100 percent as possible.

## Confronting the Cold, Honest Truth

There are multiple leadership gurus and countless leadership programs out there that all effectively claim they will get your team's health closer to 100 percent. Over the past 13 years we have delivered enough of these leadership programs to realize that while high-quality workshops, webinars, keynotes, conferences, and online curriculum are inherently good and helpful, information transfer alone does not create the lasting transformation leaders and their teams are longing for. These information transfer programs can only get the team so far and most everyone knows this to be true. Because of this, many leaders have become increasingly cynical about the latest leadership development programs, they attend fewer conferences, and read fewer leadership books than they used to. This is perfectly understandable; in fact, if you have actually read up to this point, then we congratulate you!

At GiANT, we came to the conclusion that the traditional models of leader development weren't working, and we used our own frustration and disappointment as a catalyst for change and innovation. We discovered that the classic programs were missing three foundational components:

1. A common leadership vocabulary and language that was memorable and could be used by 90 percent of the leaders inside any organization. Most programs only start at the top 10 percent and provide no transferable tools or language for the general employee population.
2. An intentional process for transferring knowledge through applied leadership learning and IQ and EQ skills into the lives of others. Event without a process leads to a rapid dissipation of impact over time.

    A personality lens that was accessible to everyone immediately, one that celebrated diversity and difference.

## Principles or Personalities?

Over the years, we've read many leadership books about building great teams, all full of generic principles like, "Learn to listen well," "Be considerate," "Give room for feedback," and so on. While we would agree wholeheartedly with such principles, we have come to the conclusion that lasting transformation only happens within a team when the leader is able to communicate using applied wisdom and where an understanding of each team member's personality and wiring is used as the filter through which the principles are communicated and applied. The 100X TEAM Program is our response to these three fundamental omissions from traditional leader development programs.

## The 100X TEAM

The 100 stands for 100 percent health in the criteria we listed earlier. Our goal is to get you and your team close to 100 percent aligned, effective, healthy, and productive. The X is about multiplication; once your team is healthy and productive we want you to have the capacity to multiply this health throughout your wider organization. We want you to multiply health, not drama; intentional leadership, not accidental leading.

X is for intentional multiplication; we've learned that if we can capture profound truth in simple visual tools, leaders can take what they've learned and train their people more effectively. The visual tools function as mirrors enabling people to see their challenges and adjust to them. When they share them with others, they learn themselves. Having begun this 100X adventure two years ago with a number of businesses, we've now proved it's possible to take the health of an executive team and multiply that health throughout the organization in a way that is liberating and empowering. When 90 percent of your organization is using the same leadership vocabulary and language to mean the same thing, at the same time, in the

**Figure 13.1   Why It Works**

same place, you will see true health multiplication (see Figure 13.1).

That is one of the reasons we wrote this book, to equip you to lead in any context, and one of the best ways to do that is to give your team the common language of the 5 Voices as well as many of the visual tools to train them to understand their voice and communicate it with precision and clarity. In essence, this is the cornerstone of our work at

> *When 90 percent of your organization is using the same leadership vocabulary and language to mean the same thing, at the same time, in the same place, you will see true health multiplication in your organization.*

GiANT: to develop a common leadership language that creates the opportunity for the honest conversations that develop more authentic relationships inside your team. It's this combination of healthy relationships, increased productivity, and intentional multiplication that defines the culture of a 100X TEAM.

The teams that win are the teams that learn to harness the gifts of their people, utilize their expertise, and train their voices in order to work together to succeed. Period.

## The GiANT Team

As we've noted before, everything we've built to share with clients has come from our own learning, from things that were a swing and a miss the first time around. Leveraging our tools, like 5 Voices, and our experience, we have worked hard to build a strong, healthy, and fully aligned team. We have joked in recent months that sometimes it feels like we're building the airplane as we fly it, but looking back at how we've spent the past 24 months launching a global message, serving clients in many countries, and training new GiANT consultants and affiliate partners, we can see the fruit of relying on tools and vocabulary as we've grown. Our team is fighting for each other's highest possible good every day, but the ability to do that didn't just happen. It has occurred because we have been intentional in learning a common vocabulary and creating a culture of empowerment and opportunity that we have found to hold up under pressure. Even when our strategy falters or, on occasion, fails, our culture holds us up because we speak the same language and share a common vision. Leaders define culture.

At GiANT headquarters, we are a mix of Pioneers, Connectors, Guardians, Nurturers, and Creatives. All of the voices are represented and we lean on all of their insights, like building the bridge and communicating change, every single day. We joke with each other frequently to keep us all loosened up and enjoying the ride, but we also see our consultants building each other up, bringing challenges, and working hard to bring their best for the greater good of the team and our larger mission. Recently, in the midst of launching some sizable initiatives, we realized as we were pioneering and creating that we hadn't effectively built the bridge for our consultants, our clients, or prospective clients.

We hadn't provided the detailed steps for our Guardians and Nurturers to walk across. We have a stable culture that allows for people to share what's not working and not hold back when there's frustration or concern. We've been able to shift into reverse, back up, and try again to communicate better and reinforce our foundational belief in the value of every member of the team. We hold ourselves up here not to suggest we're perfect, far from it, but to illustrate that the language and insights of the 5 Voices work.

In fact, we've used insights from the 5 Voices in many different ways. It has proved invaluable as a marketing tool. We have been able to tailor specific messages to reach specific voices and road test it with those we know to have that foundational voice for feedback before going live to a wider audience. Are you marketing to future-oriented voices (Pioneers, Creatives, and Connectors) or the more present-oriented conservative voices (Nurturers and Guardians)? The 5 Voices allow you to communicate with a whole new level of precision and clarity. In the same way, we have used the 5 Voices tool to place people in specific team roles that allow them to play to their strengths more often and stay in their 70/30 sweet spot. In start-up phase, it's always slightly chaotic and everyone has to roll up their sleeves and get things done, but as we've moved into the establishment phase of the business we have been able to place key leaders in seats on the bus that we know will be life giving for them, while allowing us to build foundations for future growth and expansion.

If you are ready to see real growth of your leaders inside your team as we have described, then we invite you take the 100X TEAM Challenge. It will take time to answer these questions honestly, but your answers will function as the foundation for your team's future growth and expansion.

**1. Leaders define culture! Will you commit to mastering your own voice to get to 100 percent health in the way you live and lead?**

If what we have shared in these chapters resonates with you, then we would ask you to commit to leading and living more intentionally, fighting for the highest possible good of all those you lead and influence. Taking your leadership to the next level will change the way you lead in your family, team, organization, and the wider community.

Are you willing, ready, and able to take your leadership to another level? If your answer is yes, the next step involves getting to your reality.

- Start by mastering the voice that you have discovered. Practice using your voice with your family and team.
- Will you admit what percent you are at home and work to get as close as possible to 100 percrent health and effectiveness within your leadership?

Most people desire to be the best they can be. And yet, most people need a leader to help them do that. You are that leader! When the tasks pile up and the employees whine and the budget is missed it can become difficult, but these are the moments for you to lead at another level.

**2. Will you commit to leading your team closer to 100 percent health, alignment, and effectiveness?**

Give them a chance to provide survey feedback twice a year regarding team health. Get everyone to score each of the following categories on a scale of 1 to 100 and record the data. We are sure there will be someone on your team who will enjoy collating the data and creating some charts!

- Alignment
- Synergy
- Performance
- Communication
- Capacity
- Relationships

Following one such survey, an executive team we spoke to shared that their number was 57 percent. The CEO had his score at 40 percent, and we appreciated his candor, which led to some fascinating conversations and long-term break-throughs. (This, by the way, is what it means to get to reality, being honest about the state of the team environment.) When each voice is encouraged and empowered to bring its insights, you get to a real baseline percentage for your team health very quickly. Truly listening to each other, having the honest conversations, and agreeing on plans together using the rules of engagement will move your percentage up dramatically. What would it take to get your team to 85 percent? What type of productivity and performance would that equate to? The 5 Voices will change your percentage and dramatically impact the bottom line of your team and wider organization. That is surely a discussion worth having!

**3. Will you commit to helping your team members understand their foundational voices?**

When you commit to this then you commit to becoming more intentional about the growth of your people. Think about the ideal coach: Because you know they are for you, you let them challenge and push you to be all you can be. This is the same commitment we are asking of you.

The foundational voice really does influence the way all of the other voices are experienced. The deeper teammates' understanding of their foundational voices, the better they are able to connect and communicate with the other voices on our teams. Here is how one Creative executive, CEO Ryan Underwood, describes this commitment to serving his team:

> When our executive team learned about the 5 Voices, we made some immediate staffing realignments based on the voices of our other leaders. Danielle is one of our directors and a Creative voice like mine. Carrie and Brycen recommended right away to assign her a role directly reporting to me so I would have a fellow Creative as a sounding board to prepare, season, and perfect ideas and concepts before presenting them in prime time. This has brought greater efficiency, less frustration, more process, fewer interruptions, and ushered in innovations we've wanted to make for years.
>
> We're now looking at not just skills and experience, but also natural tendencies of teammates' voices. If we have highly innovative or creative assignments, we're making sure to assign Nurturers and Guardians to teams to ensure the work gets done on time. If we're changing process or improving systems, we add Pioneers and Creatives to the team to push past barriers.

When the leader begins to help others understand their foundational voices, unparalleled team alignment and, ultimately, team performance, is not only possible, it's a probable reality.

**4. Will you commit to understanding and valuing your other teammates and their voice order?**

LV Hanson, an HR leader in Huntington Beach, California, shares his experiences to illustrate what happens when all voices are valued:

I am one of two Creative voices on a primarily Guardian executive team. I am learning that patience and strategic conversations are critical for me to help move the company forward. We are one of the most financially stable and organizationally grounded companies I've ever been a part of, but we are slower to innovate and grow. While it's comforting and safe for most, it's harder for dreamers like me. While I began with impulses of blaming and condemning, I have since learned to appreciate and celebrate the strength of the Guardians that lead our organization. The patience and strategy is not rooted in passive aggression, rather it's rooted in thankful appreciation and honor. The more I honor and express genuine gratitude for the leaders who have led us to this stable foundation, the more I can intentionally and strategically suggest ideas that might otherwise have been rejected or ignored. It's a slow process, but I'm learning to lead with gratitude, and they are learning to step out and take risks. It's a messy and beautiful relationship.

**5. Will you commit to leading your team meetings using the rules of engagement and the tools of Communicating Vision, Leading Effective Change, and Build the Bridge?**

It is not natural to have Nurturers go first in your meetings. In fact, it is very natural to be led by the pressing tasks that are right in front of you. Will you commit to applying discipline to the order in which members of your team communicate? Will you ensure that those with more lethal weapons systems use them carefully and sensitively during your team meetings? Will you commit to disciplining your internal and external communication, using the voices you struggle with as an advisory group? Will you commit to building the bridge for those voices that need the details before committing to cross the river?

**6. Will you commit to multiplying what you have learned to the entire organization? Will you work to build a bench of liberating leaders?**

The 100X TEAM is committed to raising its percentage closer to 100 and multiplying that health throughout the organization, hence the X. It starts in the Self Circle of Influence where you commit to becoming a leader worth following first. This is then multiplied throughout your team before being multiplied into the wider organization.

Every organization we know struggles with the X: there are hugely healthy executive teams that simply don't know how to multiply themselves. Multiplication is difficult with all the tasks, board meetings, daily client issues, and challenges of life that get in the way. However, by implementing the 5 Voices within your team, you are one step closer to multiplying the strength of each voice. Start there.

It took us years to figure out that traditional leader development doesn't work. We wasted a lot of money trying to figure out a better way and we believe we have found it. Sadly you can't outsource this type of transformation in your team; it has to begin in you and we'd be lying if we said it was easy. We can, however, promise we will walk with you every step of the way and help you achieve the 100X vision for your team; as GiANTs this is what we do every day and it's an incredible privilege.

The people in your life are worth it. They deserve your very best. When you lead from your foundational voice with maturity and strength, you will build a reputation of being a leader worth following. The hard work will be worth it, because in the end people will follow you because they want to, not because they have to. The world is crying out for secure, confident, and humble leaders. Will you join us in our desire to lead 100X TEAMS? If so, you will end up leading the teams and organizations everyone wants to work for!

# 14

## Change Your World

Not long ago, while we were working on this book, I (Jeremie) caught a bad cold and, in the process, lost my voice for a few days. Steve and I both spend a tremendous amount of time throughout the year traveling and speaking in the United States and in Europe, and losing my voice was a frustrating inconvenience that required a lot of rescheduling, not to mention whispered and hoarse conversations at a time of intense pressure and multiple deadlines for our growing company. Not being able to talk was exhausting, not just for me, but for everyone who found themselves on the other side of a conversation with me, in a meeting, or on the other end of a phone call.

Bad timing aside though, having laryngitis reminded me just how important it is to have a voice, to know that it's strong, and that other people can hear it. My ability to be effective in my work, with the people I lead, and with my family and friends, was seriously diminished for those few, quiet days. And when I regained my ability to talk again, it was such a relief! I no longer felt incapable or incapacitated, and I returned to my speaking engagements with renewed energy, not to mention my own aha about this larger idea of the 5 Voices that we've presented to you in these pages. We can't begin to make a difference if we don't have a fundamental understanding of ourselves. We can't be world changers if we aren't equipped for the journey.

Earlier, we introduced the idea of being intentional in understanding who you are, how you are wired, and how you speak and communicate—in raising your emotional intelligence, in other words, to be effective in all the circles of your life (see Figure 14.1). Our goal for you is to be a liberated leader who fights for the highest possible good of others. But to be able to empower the people you lead, you must first understand what it means to you personally to be liberated, because you can't give away what you don't possess. To do that, start by looking at yourself. Put your oxygen mask on first, and then you'll be able to respond to the people around you.

Being intentional is key and allows you to see the changes as they appear in yourself, your family, your team, your organization, and ultimately in your community. Why? Precisely because changes you make in your behavior create a chain reaction that causes others to begin relating to you differently. The life-altering changes in your leadership or your communication that are possible through the 5 Voices will cause a ripple effect in others. They must respond differently.

It's human nature to grow accustomed to the way people around us lead and live, and we begin to have expectations of

**Figure 14.1 5 Circles of Influence**

one another based on our behavior. However, when our behavior changes, then we must adapt and respond differently. Like the law of physics, for every action, there's an equal and opposite reaction. We hope that there are several areas in this book that spark some recognition of changes you can make to begin your own transformation chain reaction. This is how the process for changing your world for the better begins. You are the instigator.

We believe that if you develop an awareness of your voice, what it sounds like to be on the other side of you, and the value that you, at your best, bring to others, then you will create this ripple effect of change across all your circles of influence. Your ability to impact your family, your colleagues, and your wider community is directly related to how well you understand the power of your own voice. Only when you understand yourself will you be able to help others make their own voice discoveries.

As this Nurturer and executive consultant discovered, simply gaining insight into her own wiring opened the door for tremendous, transformative growth:

> My baseline assumption has long been that I am an imposter at work. Despite files of accolades and positive feedback, a consistent history of merit raises, and a "4.9 out of 5" survey average over 15 years for the effectiveness of my work, I still constantly questioned whether my work contribution was helpful or meaningful to my clients.
>
> However, once I understood that a common Achilles' heel of a Nurturer is the undervaluing of one's own contribution, I felt a sense of relief. That insight served as a sort of demystification of this confusing blend of high work competence, which was externally appreciated, coupled with the low confidence I internally experienced.
>
> This insight into my wiring has allowed me to silence the imposter's voice that I had grown so accustomed to hearing. I would compare the feeling of relief to the feeling that an Olympic sprinter must feel when she can finally shed the weight of the training parachute she has been saddled with in practice. Without that weight I can now fully tackle, and actually *enjoy*, my work in a way that I never had.
>
> Just two weeks after having this insight, I found myself in a challenging work circumstance that previously would have caused me a great deal of anxiety. This time the preparation and execution of a large presentation for an audience of 200 was a task I embraced with the confidence that is well-earned over a successful 15-year career.

That day the external quality of my delivery was the same, but internally, I enjoyed my work in a way I had not before. Silencing the imposter's voice made room for positive thinking instead of second-guessing. *Most importantly, it made room for a focus on serving others rather than being self-conscious.* The shift was remarkable given that it came from the simple insight that Nurturers often underestimate their own value, even when such feelings are not indicated.

Whether you are a Pioneer, Connector, Guardian, Creative, or Nurturer, you can only be a world changer if you are authentic and intentional. With the 5 Voices vocabulary now in your grasp, you have the tools to silence your own imposter and speak the leadership voice the world has been waiting to hear. What good words will you bring us? We are all listening.

# Transformational Leadership Resources

If you would like more information about the 5 Voices and how to apply them in your life or would like to add your story, visit www.5Voices.info.

Numerous organizations have benefited from incorporating the 5 Voices into their companies. If you would like to arrange a workshop or retreat or introduce the 100X Teams program into your organization, contact info@giantworldwide.com.

If you would like more leader resources, including workbooks, exercises, videos, or tools, contact www .giantworldwide.com/blog.

If you would like to be apprenticed to learn how to create a system to change your culture and build a team of all-stars, take a look at www.giantworldwide/xcore or contact info@giantworldwide.com to schedule a conversation.

# About GiANT
# Worldwide

GiANT Worldwide is a global transformational leadership company, focused on creating world class content and programs that help people become leaders worth following and then training them to build other leaders worth following. Our vision is to change the style of leadership around the world by training liberating leaders in every city and sector in the world.

Our secret sauce comes in our ability to train up to 90 percent of an organization, not just the top 10 percent, while creating simple, scalable, and sustainable systems for long-term organizational health.

Our specialties include:

- Teaching a common language that 90 percent of an organization can understand, use, and teach.
- Utilizing visual tools that shape culture and enhance leadership growth.
- Inserting a pass-it-on apprenticeship process into organizations that blows away traditional leadership development programs with a system that impacts culture for a decade.

- Focusing on individual transformation rather than on information transfer. We teach self-awareness that spreads throughout teams to produce secure, confident, and humble leaders.
- Serving clients in agile and relevant ways to fit the fast-paced, task-oriented work world.

To find out how to implement the 100X Teams program into your organization, or if you are interested in becoming a GiANT consultant, affiliate, or joint venture partner go to www.giantworldwide.com.

# Speaking Inquiries for Jeremie Kubicek and Steve Cockram

If you have enjoyed the content created by Jeremie Kubicek and Steve Cockram and would like to bring one or both of them to speak at your conference, organization, or event, you can contact them at:

www.jeremiekubicek.com
www.stevecockram.com
www.giantworldwide.com/speaking

Topics include:

- 5 Voices: How to Discover Your Voice, Build Your Team, and Change Your World
- 5 Gears: How to Be Present and Productive When There Is Never Enough Time
- Making Your Leadership Come Alive
- Becoming a Leader Worth Following
- And much more.

# Acknowledgments

We would like to thank the following people for work on the 5 Voices and as supporters of us throughout the book writing process.

- Thank you to our families for putting up with us writing two books in six months.
- Amy Norton, you are a rock star. Seriously. Thank you for editing this book while helping to launch 5 Gears. We are forever grateful.
- Helen Cockram, thank you for your additional eye for editing. It was perfect timing.
- A big thank you to Mike Oppedahl, Justin Westbrooks, Hunter Hodge, Amy Ferguson, and Chris Ediger for your leadership and partnership in building out an infrastructure to literally change the world!
- To all the GiANT Worldwide consultants and partners in the United States and the United Kingdom we thank you! You are amazing at what you do. This next season is going to be amazing.
- To Jeff Lamkin, Kevin Bailey, and Matthew Myers, thanks for your partnership.
- We have really enjoyed our partnership with John Wiley & Sons. Thanks to Shannon, Melissa, Deborah, Liz, Peter, and the team for all of your hard work!
- To John Cotterill, Matt Keen, and the wider Endava family who went first and helped us develop this content.

- To Michael and Lesley Anne Newman who inspired Steve to qualify in Myers-Briggs and Firo-B all those years ago. 5 Voices would not have happened without you.
- To Mike Breen, who first showed us the power of using visual tools to build an apprenticeship culture.
- Thanks to the wider GiANT family for your partnership—GiANT Capital, GiANT Partners, GiANT Experiences, and GiANT Impact.
- A special thanks to our clients for allowing us to be us in helping you be you.
- To the future cities and our future clients, we are fired up to serve you, raise up leaders, and change the way leadership occurs.
- Lastly, thank you, the reader, for discovering and mastering your voice. Build your team and watch your world change.

# Index